AF413711

BUILDING YOUR ROAD TO REMARKABLE

SIMPLE STEPS TO GREATER SUCCESS

RICHARD J. DEVRIES

ISBN paperback: 979-8-9856749-0-3
ISBN hardcover: 979-8-9856749-1-0
ISBN ebook: 979-8-9856749-2-7
ISBN audiobook: 979-8-9856749-3-4

Published by Brilliant Moves, LLC
rick@RoadtoRemarkable.com
www.RoadtoRemarkable.com

To my mom and dad, Barbara and Dean DeVries.

Thank you for giving me life, roots, wings, and love,

and for building a truly remarkable road.

Contents

Introduction

In July 2003, I walked down the stairway from the second floor of the main office of the Bank of Lenawee in Adrian, Michigan. Just a few days earlier I had accepted the position of President and CEO of the bank, and I was now heading to the lobby to address the employees for the first time.

My mind was racing as I took each step, knowing that I had no prepared remarks. Whatever I said, I felt, had to come from my heart. As I walked, my mind was searching for something to galvanize my thoughts. I needed an object or an illustration that could convey to the team the passion I felt and the potential I saw for the future. The bank was located in a small Midwestern town, and the competition was formidable, but I sincerely believed we had the capacity to flourish.

Just as I entered the lobby amid the throng of gathering team members, I saw one of our wonderful facilities managers walking toward me, and the answer to my search flashed into my mind. "Gary," I said, "do you have a hammer available?"

"Yes," he said, and he quickly pivoted away from me and headed out the door.

In just a few minutes, Gary returned with a small, lightweight hammer. I took it from his hand, thanked him, and then asked, "Do you have a bigger one? A real hefty, hearty hammer?" He smiled, pivoted again, and within moments I was holding just what I needed.

As the employee meeting began, I introduced myself and briefly reviewed the history of the bank, the community, and the competition, explaining both the challenges and opportunities that lay ahead of us. Everyone listened intently and with deep interest.

After adequately framing the situation, I paused, slowly raised the hammer, and then said, "This hammer is a symbol of why I am here and of what we are going to do. We are going to crush our weaknesses and build our strengths. In so doing, we will build the bank, build the value of the stock held by our shareholders, and build the opportunity for each of us to prosper. We will crush the competition and we will build market share. We will crush and build, hammer on, and have fun."

Within a week, each employee had a new hammer on their desk, bearing a small plaque on the handle that read, "Crush and Build. Hammer on. And have fun!" That symbol rallied the team and became a standard of performance that we aspired to achieve. We talked about the principles of crushing weaknesses and building strengths, and we took that message to our customers and prospects, presenting many of them with hammers and a card that explained their symbolism.

That symbolism led to my writing of weekly inspirational "Thursday Thoughts" that shared principles of how to crush weaknesses and build strengths. Ultimately, it led to the weekly publishing of many of those thoughts in the local newspaper. This book is the compilation and revision of these thoughts and articles.

It's about Your Road and Your Journey

If you have a desire to change—to improve—this book was written for you. It does not matter who you are, how old you are, or where you are in life's journey. It does not matter whether you are at the pinnacle of success, struggling to achieve success, or dreaming about the success that you hope to achieve. What does matter is what you do with the knowledge it contains.

I grew up in St. Joseph, Michigan, an iconic beach town on the southeastern shore of Lake Michigan. Its downtown is magical and features a brick road—State Street—that runs through a historic district of homes and continues past a delightful assortment of shops, restaurants, and boutiques.

The brick road undulates with interesting imperfections and unique dips and rises, reflecting many years of travel from residents and guests. It is distinctive, beautiful, and appreciated by all who visit this wonderful community. Extensive crushing and building was required to build this remarkable road.

Like State Street, everyone's personal road to remarkable is paved one brick at a time with a bit of crushing and building. Each brick is a virtue, a principle, a practice, or an attribute that we add to our road during the journey through life. Remarkable people are the sum of a lifetime of carefully chosen bricks, laid with labor and love.

This book is a collection of some of the most important bricks in life, with a few helpful suggestions on how they can be placed onto your road. At the end of each chapter I invite you to act. Think of this prompt as one small step to kick-start the application of the principle in your life.

As you finish a chapter, I encourage you to record your thoughts, feelings, and impressions in a journal, whether that is on paper or on a device. You will find that the more frequently you record those things, the more frequently they will come. You will find yourself writing things down that inspire you to act and stand on higher ground. The knowledge that you gain will become understanding in your heart.

Don't rush your reading. Take time to ponder the principle, write what comes into your heart and mind, then act on it. As you act on it, your understanding will lead to becoming.

Whether you are nine or ninety-nine, each day offers an irreplaceable opportunity to choose and lay the bricks that will lead to happiness and leave a legacy of success and excellence.

I wish you well on your journey.

PS: Chapters are not placed in any specific order, so feel free to read the chapter you feel drawn to each time you pick up the book. It's your choice because it's your life—and your road to remarkable.

1

How's Your Vision?

The title of this chapter might evoke thoughts about scheduling a trip to the optometrist. But as important as regularly scheduled eye exams are, that is not the vision I am referring to. Rather, it is the vision of the mind and the heart.

Remarkable accomplishments are almost always preceded by clear vision. Somewhere deep inside of us, in our mind's eye, we can see what we want to accomplish. The clearer we see it, the higher the likelihood that we will achieve it—and that often requires mental effort.

Like the astronomer who may spend months or years focusing the lenses of a high-powered telescope to find celestial bodies deep in space, we, too, must expend energy to focus the lenses of our heart and mind to gain a clear vision of what we want to achieve.

I once attended a speech given by the Olympic gold-medal gymnast Mary Lou Retton. During her presentation, she shared stories about the pain she endured every day she practiced. As I recall, when asked by someone how she endured it, the answer was she saw gold. Every day that she practiced, she imagined herself standing on the top platform, head bowed, having the gold medal placed around her neck. Her vision was clear and powerful—and it became reality.

Organizations, like people, also need vision. In fact, one of the greatest responsibilities of leaders is to create that vision and share it with others. Like an artist who conveys a vision of the world by placing paint on a canvas, leaders must likewise employ a palette of words to paint a vivid picture of the vision they see.

When we were young parents with six children, we applied this principle in our home. One evening we sat down with our little crew and asked them to imagine they were outside our home, looking into the home through the windows. We invited them to imagine what they would see, smell, feel, and experience if everything were as they desired it.

As they pondered this question, we could see the wheels spinning and were then barraged by a series of words and phrases like "wonderful aromas," "kind words," "creative learning," "clean," "treasured memories," "first things first," "fitness," "soft voices," and many more.

After reviewing all the input, we drafted a family vision, printed it out, and read it as a family every week until our children were grown. It became a standard to aspire to and source of inspiration to guide us. While we never perfectly achieved everything in the family vision, we grew closer by striving to live up to it, and those words remain a sacred part of our family memories to this day.

To be powerful, vision must come from the heart and should create in the mind of the listener an image so clear as to be unquestionable. No one questioned Mary Lou Retton's vision of her future. She closed her eyes and saw herself tumbling, balancing, and vaulting through the air and onto the gold platform. But achieving that vision included work, pain, and sacrifice, mixed with moments of perfect performance.

As your vision becomes crystal clear, it then becomes a document that is stored in your heart and reviewed repeatedly until the vision is achieved.

Now the question is this: What is your vision for you? Can you see it clearly? Have you shared it with others? Are you passionate about it? And what is the vision for the organization you own or for which you work? Does it inspire you? Does it motivate your team?

Whatever the answer to these questions, there is no doubt that vision can lead to victory. No matter who you are or what you do, it may be time to focus the lens and take a good look.

Invitation to Act

Pick any aspect of your life or any role in life that you play. Close your eyes and see yourself or your organization as you imagine things could be. When you get a clear vision of what you see, write it down. Then read it often and work to make it reality.

What are your thoughts, feelings, and impressions?

2

Go Find Your Purple Cow

One of my favorite books is *Purple Cow: Transform Your Business by Being Remarkable* by Seth Godin. In the book, Godin tells the story of how he and his family were driving through the countryside of France and were enchanted with the endless pastures filled with cows. At first, the sight of the cows was captivating to them, but after a while, they started ignoring the cows—the cows became boring. That is, of course, unless they were to see a purple cow—now that would be remarkable.

The challenge that Godin gives to his readers is to look at their organizations (and their lives) and begin to create purple cows—products and events that are remarkable and stand out in a field full of brown cows. This practice has the potential of adding value to any pursuit. Looking for the remarkable can lead to increased sales, membership, involvement, or whatever metric you hope to improve. And the pursuit can be fun. Just think about the word *remarkable*. If something is remarkable, it is worth remarking about—people talk about it.

Thus, Godin teaches the principle that ideas, like viruses, are spread by people. When someone who has a cold sneezes in a room, other people catch the cold. Likewise, when someone experiences something remarkable, they "sneeze" the idea to others, and the idea spreads like a virus.

The purple cow principle can be applied to any organization from businesses, to nonprofits, to families. The key is to do something, offer something, or be something so remarkable that people can't help but spread the news.

To further apply the purple cow principle to any organization, try applying it to people instead of products. How can you, as an employee, become a purple cow within your organization, or how can you become a purple cow as a spouse or a parent?

As a young father, I tried answering that question for myself. I had committed to prepare a small lesson for a family activity. The activity was to be followed by the eating of some treats that I agreed to pick up at the grocery store. I had worked on some thoughts for the lesson and was prepared to share them with our children. But as I drove home from work, I thought, "What could make this lesson remarkable?"

So instead of just teaching the lesson, I went home and, in fifteen minutes, made a treasure hunt that took the children on an adventure inside and outside the house. They had to follow a series of clues that led them to various locations in our home or yard, and at each location one of the principles or concepts of the lesson was hidden—along with a clue that led them to the next location.

When the treasure hunt was over, we talked about what they had learned, and then I gave them the last clue, which led them to the freezer where their treat was waiting to be eaten. The fun we had, and the delight in their eyes, told me that the ordinary had been converted into the extraordinary. The interesting point is that it took only a few minutes of typing clues and placing them in their locations to create remarkable. And there was no incremental cost, other than time, to accomplish the treasure hunt.

A few days later I had another remarkable experience. It was early on a Tuesday morning when an employee knocked on my office door and then walked in. He was holding in his hand a bag from a local fast-food restaurant.

"Good morning," I said. "What are you up to?"

"Bringing you breakfast," he replied, adding, "I saw you were here early and thought I would bring you something to eat." The breakfast was not remarkable, but his kindness was.

No matter what your roles are in life, and no matter what business or nonprofit organization you represent, go find your purple cow. With any luck, people will begin to sneeze about it, and the virus will spread.

Invitation to Act

Choose one organization you are associated with and propose a change to a product or service they offer—one that will become a purple cow to those who use the product or service. Or pick a role in life that you play and make a change to the way you perform that role that creates a purple cow experience for others.

What are your thoughts, feelings, and impressions?

3

Where Are You Going?

In Lewis Carroll's classic *Alice In Wonderland*, Alice finds herself in an engaging dialogue with Cheshire cat. The dialogue, as presented below, exposes Alice to a truth that confronts all of us.

"Cheshire Puss," she began, rather timidly, "would you tell me, please, which way I ought to go from here?"

"That depends a good deal on where you want to get to," said the Cat. "I don't much care where . . . ," said Alice.

"Then it doesn't matter which way you go," said the Cat.

What is the truth revealed to Alice? It is this—to choose a course of action, we must first know where we are going. And it is just as true for you and me as it was for Alice. Too often we choose our path without first deciding on our destination. That can result in time, money, and effort being spent in the wrong direction.

Thus, before beginning anything—whether it's a trip across the country, a meeting, or a remodeling project—it is wise to follow the counsel of author Stephen R. Covey. In his book *The 7 Habits of Highly Effective People,* Covey suggests that we always "begin with the end in mind."

Simply stated, beginning with the end in mind means that we determine our goal or destination before we begin the journey. Having our goal clearly defined serves as a filter through which all our decisions must pass. If we know where we are headed, then we will only make decisions that move us along the path to our goal.

I once attended the board meeting of a nonprofit organization. The members of the board were wrestling to determine which of many paths to take as they worked together for the good of those they served. But after a lengthy dialogue, they could not come to a consensus.

Finally, someone went to the heart of the matter and asked the question: "What do we really want to achieve or accomplish?" There was some lengthy debate over the subject, and it became clear that they really didn't know what they wanted, and it would take some additional discussion to answer that question. Accordingly, and wisely, they deferred making the decision regarding which path to follow until they first decided where they were going.

To Socrates is ascribed the quote, "Know thyself." I would add to his thought the invitation to "Know thy desired destination." Once you have made that determination, the path will become clear. Choose your goal, then choose your path. And have a wonderful journey.

Invitation to Act

Set one achievable goal for yourself, then define the path that will get you to the goal. Make sure you are committed to the goal, then go achieve it.

What are your thoughts, feelings, and impressions?

4

Be Prepared

As simple as it is, the motto historically used by the Boy Scouts of America is equally powerful. Captured in just two words, this motto offers sage counsel that can be applied to anyone, at any age, at any time: "Be Prepared."

Whether on the athletic field, in the office, or at home, and whether playing a musical instrument, making a home repair, or taking an exam at school, the following axiom always applies too: "Proper preparation prevents predictably poor performance." Or, said differently, proper preparation promotes powerfully positive performance.

In many cases, proper preparation requires more time and effort than the actual performance of a task. Take a musical recital for example. Those performing will practice, practice, and practice for a performance that lasts only a few minutes.

We once experienced the importance of proper preparation when tackling the task of painting the ceilings in the hallways of our home. About an hour or two prior to beginning the painting, my wife opened a bag of blue painting tape. We applied the tape to the walls of the hallways at the point where they met the ceiling. This allowed us to roll the paint on the ceiling without worrying about getting white paint on the walls. We likewise applied the protective tape to all the light fixtures, preventing them from being painted in the process.

The preparation process was tedious and time consuming. But without that tape, we would have spent more time touching up the walls or wiping down the light fixtures than we would have spent painting the ceiling.

My experience is that proper preparation builds confidence and reduces the fear factor. How many times have any of us gone into a meeting well prepared, feeling confident that, having done our homework, the meeting would go well? But the opposite is also true.

So here are a few items to think about prior to engaging in your next important task:

- Think through the event or task in great detail. Walk through the entire event in your mind, from start to finish, as if you were seeing it all happen. Picture the people who will be present, the materials needed, and the steps to be taken.

- As you are thinking through the event, jot down a list of the steps that come to your mind regarding the task. If you are preparing to fix the sink, for example, ask yourself what materials, tools, parts, and actions are needed. You might have all the tools assembled, but if you did not think to first turn off the water supply, you may create a larger problem.

- Don't take shortcuts. The old saying "measure twice, cut once" is so true. If you suspect you need additional materials or need to do something to be properly prepared, do it.

So often in life we only get one shot at an opportunity. Whether making the last free throw of a basketball game, doing a presentation to sell a product, delivering a talk in a public forum, or having an important conversation with a family member, always remember that proper preparation promotes powerfully positive performance. Make sure every shot you take in life has the highest probability of being right on the target by being properly prepared.

Invitation to Act

The next time you undertake any activity, task, or endeavor, take ten minutes to close your eyes and experience it as though it were happening. As you allow your mind to take you down the path to completion, write down every item you see yourself needing, using, and doing. Then take a moment to read what you've written. You may find that there are more tasks that you see in your mind's eye as you read it.

What are your thoughts, feelings, and impressions?

5

Commit to Communicate

Few things are more important in life than effective communication. Its presence can lead to tremendous success—in relationships, families, friendships, and businesses. And a lack of communication can lead to dysfunction, frustration, and failure. Communication must be honest, consistent, and frequent. The old saying, "Any news is better than no news," is so true.

It was in that spirit that I once made a commitment to our bank's employees that every Thursday I would send them a Thursday Thought email. These thoughts would range from informative to inspirational and would allow me to share—from the heart—messages that would benefit us as fellow team members.

I felt so strongly about this commitment to communicate that I made a promise to all the employees. The promise was simple—if I failed to send one of the Thursday Thought emails, I would give each employee a five-dollar bill that would come out of my pocket. It was my way of putting an exclamation point on the importance of communication. Besides, I figured that by putting my own pocketbook at risk, it would be a great incentive for me to remember to get the Thursday Thought out on a timely basis each week.

Well, about three weeks later I was sitting at my desk on a Friday morning when I realized I had not sent out a Thursday Thought the day before. It had been a busy day and I had simply dropped the ball. For a moment, I considered sitting quietly to see if anyone would notice. But then the words *commitment to communicate* came to the forefront of my thoughts, and I realized that I had only one course to follow.

Before anyone called me on it, I withdrew approximately $600 from my checking account—in the form of five-dollar bills—and hand delivered them to each of our employees. Did I regret doing it? Not for a minute (although I felt the pain).

The fact is that my credibility was on the line, and, in life, we are only as good as our word. In addition, I did learn some vital lessons from this experience. Here are a few of them:

- Be careful about what you commit and communicate to do. If you make a commitment to anyone, you better be willing to live up to it.

- Have a system in place to make sure you do what you commit to do. Note it in your calendar, have an associate remind you, or tape a message to your computer screen—whatever works for you.

- Make sure you have the resources to live up to the commitment. I did, but had I offered $100 per person, I might have needed to apply for a loan.

- Don't cry over spilled milk. When you must ante up on your commitment, have fun doing it. Seeing the smiling faces of our employees *almost* made my mistake worthwhile.

- Learn the lesson from your mistakes, and then move on. I kicked myself at least a couple of times for my mistake, but that's it. Each of us does too much good to get down on ourselves for our occasional blunders.

- Remember that the little things in life—like a five-dollar bill—count a lot. I have never seen so many people do happy dances.

Communication and commitment are critical to our success in every aspect of our lives. Communicate often, communicate clearly, and live up to your commitment to do so.

Invitation to Act

Think about the relationships in your life and determine one person—or group of people—who merit better communication from you. Make that commitment and live up to it.

What are your thoughts, feelings, and impressions?

6

Face the Facts

Have you ever been in a situation where you are asked to share your opinion on something but have not told the truth? This happens on a frequent basis in almost every organization from businesses to schools to nonprofit organizations to families.

Most frequently, we don't tell the truth for a couple of reasons: (1) we don't want to hurt someone's feelings, and (2) we are afraid of the consequences of telling the truth. Both reasons are understandable, but the truth of the matter is that a failure to tell the truth creates a situation where the successful forward progress of an organization is limited.

In his book *Good to Great*, Jim Collins uses the phrase "confronting the brutal facts." This refers to the importance of being absolutely honest with ourselves and others in assessing, evaluating, and addressing any problem or situation we may encounter. Personal or organizational dishonesty always places a roadblock in our pathway to progress and prosperity.

Take a hypothetical situation, for example, where a company employee makes a presentation that proposes a course of action to increase sales. The employee has worked on this plan for weeks, and everyone is eager to learn about it. But as the presentation is made, it is clear to everyone that the employee's facts are wrong, the plan is flawed, and it simply won't work. Yet, at the end of the presentation, to avoid conflict and to avoid embarrassing the employee, everyone compliments the employee on the excellent job and commits to help implement it. No one wanted to confront the brutal facts.

You can predict the results with 100 percent accuracy. Everyone will leave the room with no commitment to the project and no confidence in it. In the end, the project will become an exercise in futility because no one was willing to tell the truth.

The truth is that this scenario occurs daily in all our lives. Over and over again, a failure to confront the brutal facts leads to the inability to achieve real growth and positive performance.

We should all remember, though, that confronting the brutal facts does not imply behaving in a brutal fashion. It is the truth that is to be confronted, not the individual. Kindness, courtesy, and respect for each other—real caring—create an environment of trust that is necessary for people to be honest with each other.

As difficult as it is, be prepared to tell the truth—and to accept the truth—about the brutal facts of the problems and opportunities you encounter.

Invitation to Act

The next time you are in a situation where you are asked to express your opinion, tell the truth. Do it with courtesy and respect, but with honesty and clarity.

What are your thoughts, feelings, and impressions?

7

Try a Little Spring Cleaning

Springtime is refreshing and revitalizing. The birds return, the flowers and trees begin to bloom, and the number of blue-sky, sunshiny days increases in their frequency. And if you're like most people, thoughts of spring cleaning make their way to the mind as a prelude to the planting and playing that will occur in the warmer days to come.

One weekend we did some spring cleaning ourselves. Cluttered closets filled with winter clothes were emptied, organized, and restocked. The garage was likewise purged of the sand, salt, and equipment of wintertime, and a cleaner, more orderly environment emerged. When the efforts were complete, a sense of peace and satisfaction prevailed, and we all felt great.

There is something therapeutic about the process—and the results—of spring cleaning. Life always seems simpler when the clutter is removed, and we really don't have to wait until spring to do it.

The spring cleaning principle applies not only to our homes, but to our time and our lives. An effort to declutter, to separate the essential from the nonessential, to put first things first, and to simplify life, is refreshing and revitalizing.

My grandmother once told me that in life what will kill you is not the work you do, but the work that you leave undone. And she was right. I remember so clearly feeling the heaviness of heart that came because my list of to-dos was longer than the time available to do them. But if I was honest with myself, many of the essential to-dos could not be completed because I had filled my time with too many nonessentials. I had traded tasks that were important for unimportant things that seemed urgent.

I felt this so clearly one day as I came home in the early evening from some meetings. As I arrived and placed my briefcase on the floor, our nine-year-old came running up to me and invited me to come sit with him on the hammock in our backyard.

My to-do list was filled with a seemingly urgent collection of follow-up phone calls, projects around the house, and materials to read. But in this instance, wisdom prevailed, and I traded some unimportant to-dos for a moment in time with a nine-year-old that I will never forget. That decision was one of the best I made that week, and it reminded me of the need to further declutter my life so that I can better fill it with the things that bring real joy.

As you consider conducting some spring cleaning (at whatever time of year it might be), be sure to include your time and your life on the list to declutter. And make sure your to-do list has room for what matters most.

Invitation to Act

Think of one area in your life that can be decluttered and simplified, then do it and enjoy the freedom you will discover.

What are your thoughts, feelings, and impressions?

8

Developing Discipline

It seems that everyone these days is in search of a key to unlock success in life. Whether it is weight loss, hair retention, firm muscles, or increased personal income, there seems to be no shortage of quick fixes offered—for a price. Unfortunately, most of these fixes only result in a thinner wallet on the part of the purchaser, with little actual success being achieved.

The fact is that there are few shortcuts to real success in life. Most personal growth comes from paying the price of applying correct principles in a disciplined fashion. In the end, discipline and, more specifically, self-discipline, is one of the keys to success in any venture.

I had the privilege of witnessing a performance of one of the great violin virtuosos in the world, Janet Sung. A native of New York City, Sung began playing the violin at age seven and made her debut with the Pittsburgh Symphony Orchestra at age nine. She studied at the Juilliard School on a full scholarship and was serving as an assistant faculty member at the same institution. In addition, she has won numerous national and international awards and is as delightful as she is talented. She performed in Adrian, Michigan, with the Adrian Symphony Orchestra, and it was truly a night to remember.

Regarding her performance in Adrian, *The Daily Telegram* newspaper remarked, "Whether you were hearing this piece [Vivaldi,

"The Four Seasons"] for the first time or the 500th, Sung's bravura work was enough to put you on the edge of your seat. It certainly earned her every bit of the lengthy (and wildly enthusiastic) standing ovation she received."

Prior to her performance, my wife, Dyana, and I had an opportunity to listen to her speak to a small group of guests. On that occasion, someone asked Sung what price she had paid to become the great violinist that she is. Her response was stunning to everyone in the room.

She explained that her high school yearbook contains one page that is dedicated entirely to her—to the one day in her high school career that she didn't practice violin from the time school was over to the time she went to bed (except for homework and dinner). She then described the daily routine of intense practice that occurred from the time she began playing violin, until the day we met with her.

For the better part of her life, Janet Sung sacrificed the luxury of free time, relaxation, and being with friends to practice the violin. It was a lifetime of self-discipline, resulting in an achievement of world-class expertise.

Self-discipline is what separates dieters from weight losers, top performers from daydreamers, and, often, winners from losers. It is the gold standard of Olympic champions, the common denominator of achievers, and the separator of good intentions from great achievements.

Whether you want to lose weight, learn a new talent, prosper in your work, obtain better grades, or overcome a bad habit, self-discipline is an indisputable (and often painful) key that will help open your personal door to success. The great mountain climber, Sir Edmund Hillary, said it best: "It is not the mountain we conquer, but ourselves."

Whatever your dream or endeavor, add self-discipline to the equation and enjoy the results.

Invitation to Act

Examine one area of your life where you are struggling to achieve a goal and consider how focusing on self-discipline in that area will help you. What could you achieve if you were consistent in pursuing the goal? Write down your commitment to act and then do it.

What are your thoughts, feelings, and impressions?

9

Change Yourself First

We all frequently want to change the behavior of those around us. Whether it is the behavior of a spouse, a child, a team, a group of employees, or a friend, we all find ourselves wanting others to raise the bar—to change. The question is how to accomplish that, particularly when the only behavior we have control over is our own?

True, we can force others to change, but that usually results in a change of actions, not in a change of heart—and the change is rarely permanent. The same is true when we try to bribe someone to change by offering rewards and accolades for the desired results.

The ironic and powerful truth facing all of us is that we have the greatest effect on changing the behavior of others by changing ourselves. Gandhi, who led India to independence from Great Britain, said it best: "We must become the change we want to see."

That statement is an invitation to lead by example and to sacrifice comfort to gain commitment. In his 2000 book *Change the World,* author Robert E. Quinn tells the following story about the legendary Boston Celtics basketball player, Larry Bird:

> As the 1984 season began, Bird was obsessed with winning the championship that had eluded his team in 1982 and 1983. In recalling that year, his teammates

describe the extent of Bird's dedication. He would arrive on the practice floor an hour and a half early and stay an hour afterwards. During this time he would discipline himself, running drills and practicing the basic aspects of his game. Although Bird never said a word about it, the rest of the players soon followed his example. As the season started, Bird continued to set the example of self-discipline and self-sacrifice. He continually extended himself, throwing himself into the crowd in pursuit of loose balls, taking painful charges on defense, and generally hustling on every play. Again, Bird said nothing, yet the other players were soon doing the same. The Celtics ended up with the best record in the league and had little difficulty getting to the championship series.

Based on Larry Bird's willingness to lead by example and to become better than he was, the team followed his example, and *they* became better. Ultimately, in one of the most remarkable tournaments in basketball history, the Boston Celtics won the NBA championship.

What is the lesson to be learned? The answer is as painful as it is simple—to help others change we must first be willing to change ourselves.

Change for the better is rarely convenient, is often uncomfortable, and always requires that we make a sacrifice. But if the price is paid, the performance improves, and the playing field rises to new levels.

Before you ask someone to go the extra mile, to work harder, to play with more heart, or to soar to loftier heights, stop and ask yourself if you are willing to go there first. Chances are that if you do, others will follow you. By changing yourself, you will have changed the world around you.

Invitation to Act

The next time you hope to change someone else's behavior, or to help an organization change for the better, ask yourself what changes you are willing to make first.

What are your thoughts, feelings, and impressions?

10

Innovate to Invigorate

I once had an interesting conversation with a dairy farmer while he gave me a tour of his facility. At the end of the tour, he paused to make a request that caught me by surprise. His request was this: "Tell me about the role of innovation in your company." That request led to a wonderful dialogue that has caused me to reflect on the importance of innovation and the invigoration that it brings into our lives.

The dictionary defines innovation as "the introduction of something new . . . a new idea, method, or device." Truly, innovation is the ability to create and do things differently in a way that differentiates a business, organization, or person from others.

I met with a customer who had designed and developed a piece of equipment that was unique to his industry. It allowed him to operate at a lower cost than his competitors. This translated into increased profits and a higher probability of long-term survival. There is no doubt that innovation benefits the bottom line.

And innovation invigorates. While change is never easy, it can be the shot in the arm that breathes enthusiasm into any organization. Innovation stimulates the mind and inspires the heart. Innovative ideas start the adrenaline pumping and can give energy and purpose to any business. And innovative ideas have saved more than a handful of dying companies.

But when it comes to innovation, it helps to get as many people involved as possible. In fact, after I discussed innovation with the dairy farmer, he asked me another question: "Who is responsible for innovation in your company?" My response was everyone.

Each person has a different background, perspective, and viewpoint and can innovate. Innovation is not a function of title or position—it is a function of attitude and enthusiasm.

However, innovation does mean taking risks. There is a price to pay for innovation. It often involves cost, and it always takes courage.

In the words of Alan Kay, "The best way to predict the future is to invent it." Therefore, go innovate and invigorate your way to success.

Invitation to Act

What is one area of your life where innovation—finding a new way to do things—would lead to greater success? Spend some time brainstorming and talking to others about what those changes might be and how you might make them.

What are your thoughts, feelings, and impressions?

11

Timing Is Everything

As a boy, I used to race sailboats with my dad. The start of the race was always signaled by the firing of a cannon on an anchored motorboat at an established time. Our goal was to make sure that the bow (or front) of our sailboat was right at the starting line when the cannon went off.

If you crossed the line before the cannon fired, you had to sail around the motorboat and restart the race. If you were too far behind the starting line when the cannon went off, you ran the risk of giving away a good starting position to one of the competing sailboats. The key was waiting patiently for the right moment to trim your sails and speed ahead to the starting line, arriving there in the split second that the cannon was fired.

The many trophies won by my dad during those years serve as a reminder to me of his willingness and ability to be patient and well-timed in trimming the sails and starting the journey.

The truth of the matter is that, in life, timing is everything. Whether you are swinging a golf club or a baseball bat, buying or selling a home, investing in the stock market, making a job change, or entering a new relationship, timing is everything. You simply must be patient enough to wait for the right pitch, the right job offer, the right buyer for your home, or the right opportunity to establish a meaningful relationship.

Stacey Charter, an author, summed it up this way: "Life is all about timing . . . the unreachable becomes reachable, the unavailable become available, the unattainable . . . attainable. Have the patience, wait it out. It's all about timing."

A company waits for the right moment to introduce a new product. Parents wait for the right moment to have a heart-to-heart talk with a child. The basketball coach waits for the right moment to try a new play out on the court. All around us, every day, some of the most important decisions we make involve choosing the right timing for actions that need to be taken.

In today's fast-paced world we frequently face the temptation to trade terrific timing for quick convenience. And if we succumb to that temptation, we run the risk of trading something great for something good.

The wisdom to wait is a word to the wise that has been shared for centuries. Be patient. Make sure your timing is right. By taking the time to make timing count, you'll gather more trophies and sail the journey of life with greater success.

Invitation to Act

The next time you undertake any activity, task, or endeavor, ask yourself if the timing is right, or if you are acting impatiently. Be honest with yourself and make sure that impatience is not forcing timing that is less than optimal.

What are your thoughts, feelings, and impressions?

12

Do Things on Purpose

Have you ever done something accidentally, but were accused of doing it on purpose? The truth of the matter—and the subject of this chapter—is that we all need to do more things (good things) on purpose and add more purpose to the things that we do.

According to the dictionary, the word *purpose* means "something set up as an object or end to be attained." In other words, a purpose is a goal that we are working to achieve. Thus, to do something on purpose means to intentionally engage in actions designed to accomplish that purpose.

Given the fact that we only have twenty-four hours in each day, it is critical that we effectively use our time to accomplish our purposes or goals. The following are some ideas that may allow you to get more done in the same amount of time:

- Establish a purpose for every activity. Ask yourself the question, "When this meeting, event, or activity is done, what outcomes do I desire and what things do I hope to accomplish?" Before beginning a meeting or any activity, think it through. Make sure you (and those attending the meeting) know what you want to accomplish.

- Use your time to achieve more than one purpose. For example, let's say you are holding a meeting to train your staff on a new product. The purpose or goal is to make sure that each employee understands the product well enough to sell it. But let's also say that one of your new employees has been struggling with confidence. You might use the same training time to publicly praise that employee's efforts or to share some observations about outstanding projects the employee has done. By so doing, you have added a new purpose and dimension to the meeting. In effect, you're killing two birds with one stone. The reality is, if thought through carefully, much of our time can be used to simultaneously accomplish many important purposes.

- Make sure to take advantage of the downtimes that you have. So much of our time seems to be spent driving, traveling, waiting for meetings to start, and so on. But by adding some purpose to the equation, downtime can be converted into purposeful time.

  For example, imagine that you must run an errand to the hardware store on a Saturday morning. Your purpose is to buy a new lock for a cabinet. Well, instead of just hopping in the car and heading out, what if you used the trip as an opportunity to catch the news, listen to a chapter of a recorded book, or spend time with a spouse (or significant other) or one of your children? Adding a stop to get an ice cream cone—just for the fun of it—would add an additional purpose to the trip.

If you are like me, life is an exciting whirlwind of activity and opportunity filled with the challenges of getting more done in less time. By adding purpose to preparation, we can accomplish more, learn more, enjoy more, and better help those around us. Now go do something—on purpose.

Invitation to Act

Pick one task, activity, or meeting that you hope to undertake, and ask yourself if you have clearly identified the purpose of that endeavor. Examine ways to accomplish more than one objective while pursuing it.

What are your thoughts, feelings, and impressions?

13

Kindness Counts

Some time ago I joined a group of businesspeople from throughout the United States for dinner. These were successful individuals, both academically and professionally, who had spent their lives learning how to effectively sell their products and services to customers across the country.

At one point our host asked each of us to share our best and worst shopping experience within the previous thirty days. I listened earnestly as each guest recounted the remarkable things they had experienced at local or national restaurants, department stores, construction companies, or retail establishments.

What stunned me was the fact that every story told had nothing to do with sales techniques or methodologies. Rather, every story focused on the care and kindness that was demonstrated by the salesperson.

The guests I dined with were highly educated, financially successful, and held positions of prominence within their respective industries. They were experienced in their industry and each managed, tracked, monitored, and motivated large sales forces. But in the end, what touched their wallet was the thing that had touched their heart—kindness.

One guest told the story of calling a hotel to make reservations for a tenth wedding anniversary, The person at the hotel who took his call asked what kind of car he drove and requested the license number. He also asked about the purpose of the visit. The guest was a bit surprised, if not perturbed, at having to give the information, but complied with the request.

However, on the day of his arrival at the hotel, the valet opened the door and said to the guest and his wife, "Welcome to our hotel, and happy tenth anniversary to both of you." When the guest and his wife opened the door to their room, they found a fresh bouquet of flowers, some fresh fruit, and refreshments—all in honor of their anniversary.

Somebody had cared enough to be kind. Can you guess where the couple was headed for their eleventh anniversary?

Coincidentally, just before going to the dinner that evening, I received an email from one of our employees. Here is part of that that message, edited by me:

> Rick, I always hear you talk about all these great businesses that give excellent customer service. Well, I have received some excellent customer service that I wanted to share with you. I was doing some shopping last week, and I went to several stores and made some purchases. However, one store stood out in my mind—a women's clothing store.
>
> I made my purchase as usual, went up to pay, but instead of the sales associate handing me my purchases across the counter, she put all my items neatly in a bag and walked around the counter to hand it to me. She shook my hand, thanked me for my business, and invited me back.
>
> It did not take her any more time to walk around [the counter] and it really made an impression on me that I won't forget. I will definitely return to do more shopping.

What I want to emphasize is the employee's last comment: "I will definitely return to do more shopping." What a powerful lesson there is in this. Our employee, along with the table of dinner guests, did not notice the *sales*-ability of the stores at which they shopped. What they noticed was the *service*-ability of those who waited on them. They noticed the care and the kindness rendered to them, resulting in a desire to return.

The adage commonly attributed to Teddy Roosevelt is, and always will be, true: "People don't care how much you know until they know how much you care." The challenge for all of us, whether in business or in our personal lives, is to remember that in any interaction we have with others, kindness really counts.

Invitation to Act

In the next twenty-four hours, find a way to show a special kindness to someone you interact with.

What are your thoughts, feelings, and impressions?

14

Let's Go Do Hard Things

This chapter is an invitation to become uncomfortable, at least for a moment, by choosing to do hard things. In our lives, each of us passes through a multitude of fiery trials. We all face health, family, and employment challenges. We may also face struggles on the athletic field, in our pursuit of academic advancement, or in the preparation and performance of an artistic endeavor.

And if each of us is truly honest, the most sacred chapters of our lives are not the ones that reflect ease or easiness. Rather, the gems of our lives are those times when we faced adversity, when we did hard things, and when we endured. I have read and reread many of those painful journal entries of my life, and they are the most precious to me.

Doing hard things almost always results in tremendous growth—physically, mentally, emotionally, or spiritually. J. Willard Marriott summed it up nicely with these words: "Good timber does not grow with ease. The stronger the wind, the stronger the trees."

In that regard, I once had a tender conversation with a friend who had endured and overcome a significant health problem. The comment he made to me was, "I would not want to go through this again, but I am grateful that I did—it has changed my life." His response to his problem, because of his great attitude, was to allow the winds of difficulty to strengthen him and help him to grow.

While many hard experiences come along because of circumstances beyond our control, we don't have to wait for someone or something to act upon us to experience growth. Rather, each of us can create our own seasons of growth by proactively choosing to do hard things.

For example, one of our sons voluntarily joined both the middle and high school wrestling teams and was determined to learn and do his best. While he lost some matches based on points, he was determined not to lose by being pinned. Each time he was about to be pinned, he would arch up and support his and his opponent's weight with his neck—a very hard thing to do! Over time, he grew stronger, learned new techniques, and became very successful.

A good friend of ours chose to switch careers at age forty-nine. He had been a world-renowned pediatric cardiologist but had always dreamed of becoming a world-class chef. So, he matriculated into programs at two of the finest culinary schools in America, followed by a six-month program in France. He ended up owning and operating an extraordinarily successful catering company in the San Francisco Bay Area. Was it hard? You bet. But ask him whether it was worth it or not, and I know what you will hear.

Please remember, however, that doing hard things does not necessarily require that we do huge things. Apologizing to a friend, making a difficult phone call, or tackling a distasteful or challenging task will stretch the soul and lead to growth. So will writing thank-you letters, learning a new language, or disciplining yourself to get up a half-hour earlier every day to read a book or study a topic. In fact, I read about a local physician who woke up at 4:30 a.m. each day to write a book—definitely a hard thing.

Reflect on the hard things you've done in the past, bask in the recollection of the feelings and growth you've experienced, then decide what you can do now—something hard—that will allow you to experience them again. Let's go do hard things.

Invitation to Act

Pick an attribute you would like to obtain, a skill you would like to develop, or an important action that you feel you should undertake but haven't because it is hard—and tackle it, starting today.

What are your thoughts, feelings, and impressions?

15

Listen with Your Heart

In today's fast-paced, high-energy, long to-do list world, we all run the risk of moving so quickly that we don't take time to listen to what surrounds us.

One summer evening our family sat outside in our backyard and enjoyed some memorable moments together. We laughed, chatted, and roasted marshmallows over the fire and enjoyed the beauty that surrounded us. And much of the beauty of the evening was discovered as we listened, in our moments of silence, to the symphony of sound that surrounded us.

All around us were the melodies of frogs, crickets, bats, and birds, each singing their own song and telling their own story. The crackling, comforting sounds of the burning logs in the fire pit added a rich depth to nature's orchestral performance.

Life is often like that. We can only hear when we take the time to listen. And too often we only listen with our ears, and not with our hearts.

Listening *with* the heart requires listening *to* the heart, not just to the words we hear. So often we are in such a hurry to get the message that we don't take the time to really listen to the messenger. For true communication to take place, heart must speak to heart.

A number of years ago, as a young father, I had an experience that illustrated this principle. We were eating dinner, and one of our children refused to eat his meal. We gently worked with him, encouraging him to eat, but nothing we said convinced him to take even a bite. Finally, knowing he was scheduled to attend a roller-skating party later that evening, we told him that if he would not eat his food, he could not attend the party.

But not even that consequence affected his decision. In fact, as soon as we explained the consequence, he said that he was all done and asked if he could be excused. I asked him if he understood the consequence—that he could not go roller-skating—and he assured me that he did. Then off he went to his room.

Knowing how much he loved to roller skate, I sat there confused and dumbfounded that he would let such a wonderful opportunity slip by, especially when the meal that he had been served was one that he normally enjoyed.

It just didn't make sense. And then it hit me. I had heard his words but had not listened to his heart. He had said, "I don't want to eat my food," but that was not the message that his heart was conveying. I had missed a deeper message.

I called him back into the kitchen and invited him to sit on my lap. I held him closely, rubbed his back, and then asked him, "Is there something that is bothering you about going to the roller-skating party tonight?" And then the tears began to flow.

Amid the little sobs and the steady flow of tears, he explained that the last time he had been roller-skating, some older boys had repeatedly pushed him down. Because of that incident, he was afraid to go roller-skating, but was too embarrassed to tell us. So, he intentionally did not eat his meal in hope that we would prevent him from going roller-skating. His words had masked the message of his heart, and only true listening allowed the message to be heard.

Since then, I am sure that many such messages have been conveyed and missed, but I, like all of us, keep trying to improve.

Life is face-paced and there is normally too much on all our plates. But amid the flurry of activity and the sounds that surround us, true communication is best achieved by taking the time to listen to the whispers that can only be heard with the heart.

Invitation to Act

In your next communication with someone, ask yourself if you are really understanding what is in their heart. Seek to understand what is motivating them, what their true needs are, and how best to respond to those needs.

What are your thoughts, feelings, and impressions?

16

Make Your Own Declaration

July 4, 1776, marks the day that the thirteen colonies in North America announced their intent to separate from British rule and form the United States of America. Their intent was formalized by the publication of the Declaration of Independence, which was ratified by the Continental Congress on that same day. The official document was later signed by fifty-six men who, in so doing, pledged to support their declaration with "Our lives, our fortunes, and our sacred honor."

Each year we celebrate the establishment of that document, the formation of this country, and the liberties and privileges that we, as Americans, enjoy. We should all be forever grateful for the bravery of those individuals who were willing to give everything for the achievement of their dreams.

One of the signers of the Declaration of Independence was the president of the Continental Congress, John Hancock. He was the first to sign the document and did so with a bold, even flamboyant signature. As he signed the document, he stated, "The British ministry can read that name without spectacles." In other words, John Hancock wanted to boldly declare his support and signed the document in such a way that his signature, and the statement made by his signature, could not be mistaken. He wanted the world to know where he stood, and the ink of his pen drew the line in the sand.

My question for you today is this: what is your declaration, and are you willing to boldly sign it and declare it to the world? Whether you are a father, mother, son, or daughter, whether you own a business, work for someone, or are retired, and whether you are young or old, each of us has the right and the freedom to choose what we will accomplish and what we will become. What is your declaration?

Making a declaration to do something is at the foundation of all progress for organizations and individuals, and it requires that (1) you know where you want to go, and (2) you are willing to publicly declare your intent.

Such was the case with President John F. Kennedy who, in the early 1960s, publicly stated that the United States would put a man on the moon in that decade. And we did.

Writing down your own declaration is the first step toward achieving it. Whether it is overcoming a bad habit, starting a new business, turning around a relationship, or developing a new skill. Take the first step by making your declaration to do so.

Invitation to Act

Make the decision to do or accomplish something, however large or small it may seem. Then, write down your declaration to do so, sign it, and share it with someone you love and trust.

What are your thoughts, feelings, and impressions?

17

Never Give Up

On October 29, 1941, Sir Winston Churchill, the great political leader, orator, and prime minister of the United Kingdom, delivered a talk to the boys at Harrow School. It was given during World War II, at a time when the future of the United Kingdom, and the free world, was in the balance.

In the talk, he declared: "Never give in, never give in, never, never, never, never—in nothing, great or small, large or petty—never give in except to convictions of honor and good sense."

In a world where challenges abound and quitting is easy, this is a reminder that perseverance pays. Albert Einstein, the celebrated scientist-genius once said, "It's not that I'm so smart, it's just that I stay with problems longer."

Whether it is overcoming a trial, authoring a book, starting a business, developing a new relationship, learning to play a musical instrument, obtaining a college degree, or achieving an athletic accomplishment, keep going, hang in there, don't ever give up.

A wonderful Japanese proverb underscores this invitation: "Fall seven times, stand up eight." I witnessed a heroic example of this perseverance a number of years ago when our oldest daughter was about seven years old. She had signed up to participate in a talent show at church and had chosen a difficult song to sing.

When her moment to perform arrived, she began to sing the song with great skill and enthusiasm. But halfway into her performance, she came to an abrupt halt, having forgotten the words. As she stood there straining her memory, the music stopped, and a hush fell across the room. To our surprise, she turned to the pianist and said, "I will start over." And she did—only to hit the same brick wall a second time.

Tears flowed as she stood there—embarrassed and frustrated—but she did not give up. For the third time she began the song from the beginning, only to encounter the same problem once again. With head hung low, and amid sobs, she stood there, frozen in the moment, wrestling to find words that would not come.

At this point Dyana and I rushed forward and, wanting to relieve her pain, assured her that she did not have to continue. We praised her for the courage she had already demonstrated. But she heard another voice, the voice of her heart, that echoed the words, "Don't give up."

Well, try she did, not once more, but three or four times more. It was on the sixth or seventh try that she finally got it, and she sang the song with pure, unbridled, seven-year-old bliss from start to finish. I will never forget the look of satisfaction on her face for having triumphed over her challenge.

That determination to persevere paid off, for she went on to become an accomplished vocalist and soloist, traveling and performing in nearly all the countries of Europe throughout her high school years.

Whatever your goal, stick to it. Whatever your dream, dream on. Whatever your ambition, pursue it until it is yours. Stand firm, let the winds blow and never, never, never give up.

Invitation to Act

The next time you are tempted to abandon an endeavor—to give up—don't. Keep your eye on the goal and press forward.

What are your thoughts, feelings, and impressions?

18

No Excuses

Florence Nightingale is well known in history as the lady with the lamp. Born in 1820, she was the daughter of wealthy parents who wanted her to become a socialite and live a life of ease. Nightingale, on the other hand, had a different agenda.

Ultimately, she became a renowned nurse who, during the Crimean War, went to the battlefield and worked in filthy hospital conditions. It was there that during late night hours she was constantly seen carrying a lamp as she tended to the needs of the wounded. It was under these difficult circumstances that she revolutionized the practice of nursing, identifying the importance of hygiene in patient care and in the prevention of the spreading of disease.

When queried about her success, Florence Nightingale was quoted as saying the following: "I attribute my success to this: I never gave or took an excuse."

The world today is full of excuses. And excuses are such an easy way out since they transfer responsibility and guilt to someone or something else.

It is so easy to make an excuse, and it is often difficult to accept responsibility for mistakes. But in the end, excuses weaken our foundation of credibility and open the door to failure down the road.

On the other hand, taking responsibility for one's own actions, and not relying on excuses, results in an increase in the value of your personal stock and opens the door to opportunity.

I witnessed this latter scenario in a board meeting of an organization for which I once served as a board member. An individual had been invited to make a presentation to the board of directors in which he would ask for approval of some recommended actions.

However, in the middle of the presentation, he found it necessary to confess the need to ask for approval of an action that he had already taken. In other words, he had put the cart before the horse; he had acted without the proper authority to do so.

Rather than making a list of excuses for how and why this mistake had happened, he simply said words to this effect: "I erred in making this decision. I made the mistake and I apologize for it."

And what was the reaction of the board? You can probably guess. Though disappointed in his decision, they warmly received his apology, expressed their continued support of his work, and asked him to continue with the presentation. In that moment, his value to the board of directors went up—his personal stock price increased.

Had he presented a litany of excuses for the mistake, just the opposite would have happened. The trust placed in him would have decreased and criticism of his actions would have abounded. His personal stock would have taken a significant plunge.

In the end, no one really likes excuses, and everyone admires those who avoid them. Florence Nightingale was spot on. Never give or accept an excuse.

Invitation to Act

The next time you are tempted to make an excuse for something you said or did, don't do it. Resist the temptation, take accountability, fix things as best as you can, and move on.

What are your thoughts, feelings, and impressions?

19

One Brick at a Time

Regardless of when you read this, you, like so many of us, may be wrestling with the ongoing challenge of broken New Year's resolutions.

In many respects, New Year's resolutions—or any resolutions—are often like drops of water on a scalding hot pan. They pop, sizzle, and then evaporate in a matter of moments.

If we are all honest with ourselves, most resolutions never make it past the good intention phase. Somewhere between desire and action the enthusiasm fades and we return to the old behaviors we have become accustomed to.

The truth is, changing behavior does require tremendous energy. Like a rocket struggling to break free from the pull of earth's gravity, effort is required to break free from the powerful pull of past habits. The key to success is to not do too much all at once. The great English poet Robert Browning summed it up nicely by saying, "Less is more."

Whatever time of year it may be, instead of setting fifteen resolutions, start with just one meaningful one. Give careful thought to your selection, as if you were choosing the perfect gift to give to a dear friend or loved one.

And you are. Whatever good you are striving to accomplish will benefit the lives of those around you. Personal growth somehow always seems to have positive collateral consequences.

In selecting your one resolution, here are a few thoughts that may be of help to you. First, make it realistic. It's okay to stretch a bit, but don't try to eat the elephant in one sitting. Second, share your resolution with those around you. Like it or not, some public accountability really does help. Finally, have fun with it. As hard as change is, it is good. And when you achieve your resolution, celebrate your success. Then set another one. Remember, every road to remarkable is built one brick at a time.

Invitation to Act

Pace yourself and use wisdom as you set goals and resolutions. Rome wasn't built in a day, and you aren't either. Start with one important goal today and press forward until it is achieved. Then set another. Work hard, be patient, and lay one brick at a time.

What are your thoughts, feelings, and impressions?

20

Passion Persuades

No matter what we are doing in life, and no matter who we are interacting with, we are all engaged in the process of persuasion. The retail merchant wants to persuade people to shop at their store, the members of a city council want to persuade businesses to move into their community, and a candidate wants to persuade voters to elect them to public office. No matter who you are, you are involved daily in the process of persuasion.

While many factors can affect the process of persuasion, Anita Roddick, founder of The Body Shop, provided a great starting point with her words: "Passion persuades."

I once experienced the persuasive power of passion during a visit to a newly opened barbeque restaurant. I had been invited to visit and tour the restaurant by the owner, who was excited about sharing his vision and accomplishments. As we arrived, we walked through the lobby, the dining area, and into the kitchen, hearing the story of the restaurant as we walked. The story was impressive, as were the decorations and the ambiance. And it smelled delicious.

As we walked through the kitchen, the chef (Chef Jimmy) was introduced to us, and I could see in his eyes the passion for what he was doing. He walked up to me, shook my hand, and asked if I would like to taste some of the food. I felt like a kid in a candy shop and responded with a resounding "Yes." Within minutes I was seated with a plate in front of me and with the chef at my side.

As I began to take the first bites, he enthusiastically began to describe how everything in the restaurant—except the butter and the ice cream—were made entirely from scratch. The sauces, the bread. Everything was homemade.

As he continued, he described the slow cooking process used to tenderize and flavor the meat. He shared the detailed process of creating and testing new recipes. "We even make our own pickles," he added, describing the ingredients and process for doing so.

With each word he shared, the food and the flavors became more delightful, and the tastes became more tantalizing. I found myself savoring each bite, armed with an understanding of the process and the passion each dish was prepared with.

At one point, the chef put his hands on his knees, leaned forward, and said, "I love what I do. This is my life—to make people happy by doing what I do." Well, my dining experience was remarkable, and I concluded that I had been *passionized*. That may not be a word in Webster's dictionary, but it describes what happens when we feel the passion that someone has for someone or something.

No matter what you are attempting to build, start, or achieve, and no matter who you need to persuade to accomplish it, remember that passion persuades.

Invitation to Act

As you embark on any initiative, ask yourself if you are truly passionate about it. If not, what changes need to be made for you to feel that passion? And when you do feel that passion, share it with others. Let your passion be something that persuades them to join your cause.

What are your thoughts, feelings, and impressions?

21

The Price of Loyalty

Few qualities seem to have greater value to businesses—or relationships—than loyalty. A loyal customer returns repeatedly and provides a steady flow of revenue for a business. A loyal friend remains at your side through thick and thin, helping you to weather the many challenges of life.

But no matter what the business or relationship may be, loyalty always has a price, and that price rarely has anything to do with money. In fact, in his book *What Clients Love*, Harry Beckwith included a chapter titled, "Money Can't Buy You Loyalty." In this chapter, Beckwith shares the following insights: "Loyalty marketing often fails, however, because too many of its practitioners assume that people feel loyal to companies. They do not. People feel loyal to people . . . Loyalty doesn't come from marketing. It comes from personal sacrifice."

Beckwith's insight is as difficult to live up to as it is true. In this fast-paced world, we often try to obtain loyalty without being willing to pay the price for it. Why? Because personal sacrifice is rarely easy or convenient and requires the commitment of one of our rarest commodities—time.

I once had an experience with a local business that won *my* loyalty. It was a heating and air conditioning firm whose name and number was displayed on the central heater in our home. I had never called them before, but at 8:30 p.m. one frosty winter evening, our heater stopped working, so I gave the business a call using their emergency number.

The gentlemen I spoke to was kind and courteous and allowed me to explain my problem. After doing so, he told me what he believed the problem was, and asked if I would like to try to fix it myself. I hesitatingly said, "Yes," while harboring legitimate fears that I might only make the problem worse.

Then, to my relief, he began to lead me through the process, describing in careful detail the steps to take. His words created a visual map for me to follow, and he offered the necessary encouragement, warnings, and tips to make the process easier. Word by word, step by step, he remained with me on the phone until the job was done, and he never earned a penny for doing it. By sacrificing his time and talents in such a kind, thoughtful way, he solved my problem, earned my profound gratitude, and, yes, my loyalty.

Evaluate your relationships, spend some time and some effort, and pay the price of personal sacrifice. Do this, and you'll be on your way to reaping the rewards of true loyalty.

Invitation to Act

Pick one relationship that is important to you and ask yourself what you could do to strengthen it. What act of service or what sacrifice of time and effort should you make to deepen the relationship and earn the loyalty you desire?

What are your thoughts, feelings, and impressions?

22

Loose Lips Sink Ships

Nearly everyone has heard the phrase "Loose Lips Sink Ships," but not everyone knows the origin of those words. To the best of my knowledge, they were coined during World War II, when the United States government had serious concerns about the enemy gaining information about US military strategy, tactics, locations, and movement.

Occasionally, a soldier would innocently write home regarding the war and upcoming military activities. Then, if the letter was intercepted, or if the soldier was captured while still carrying the letter, the information could be used against our soldiers.

Hence, during World War II, posters were displayed throughout the country that read, "Loose Lips Might Sink Ships." There were other posters of similar content, with one reading, "A Careless Word . . . A Needless Sinking."

In this chapter, I would like to put a different slant on "Loose Lips Sink Ships." This slant focuses not on the risk of sharing top secret military information, but on the pain and pitfalls of speaking without first thinking. For the truth is, many ships—relation*ships*, that is—have been sunk by virtue of a thoughtless comment or an unkind word.

When it comes to relationships—whether business, professional, or personal—no torpedo has more power to sink the ship than the torpedo of the human tongue. Truly, the tongue is not only a torpedo, it is also a double-edged sword that can cause either harm or harmony. The choice is always ours.

You and I have experienced both sides of this sword. It won't take too much effort to remember being at either the sending or receiving end of a harsh word, a sarcastic comment, or an insult. And whether we were the victim or the offender, we always wish it wouldn't have happened.

But we can also remember a time when, while biting our tongue (sometimes nearly off), we thought before we spoke and filtered anger through the strainer of kindness. Such restraint usually prevents relationships from sinking and turns swords or torpedoes into tenderness. Then, instead of crushing relationships, we build them. Instead of sinking them, we insure their continued successful sailing.

As you work to build your relationships, bite your tongue, think before you speak, and remember that while "Loose Lips Sink Ships," kind words, well chosen, will soften hearts, lift spirits, heal wounds, and bring joy to both the giver and the receiver.

Invitation to Act

The next time you are tempted to say something you might regret, don't. Rather, pause, think, and choose the higher road.

What are your thoughts, feelings, and impressions?

23

Rowing in the Same Direction

Most of us have heard the familiar saying, "Let's make sure we're all rowing in the same direction." It conjures up images of a raft or rowboat full of people, each rowing in different directions. The result is predictable: little forward progress and great frustration.

I once had the opportunity to experience this while whitewater rafting down a level 3–4 river in Pennsylvania. For those of you not familiar with river ratings, the scale is from 1 to 6, with 6 being non-navigable (extremely dangerous). As it was, the river we were on was challenging, and a few people had lost their lives at one point on the river called Dimple Rock.

Dimple Rock is an ominous rock protrusion (about six feet high, ten feet long, and eight feet wide) in the middle of the river. Underneath the surface of the water, the rock has a large indentation—or dimple—that can trap you if you are unfortunate enough to hit the rock and flip your raft.

The good news is that of the eighteen rafts in our group, no one was injured, and no one lost their life. Our raft sailed smoothly to the right of Dimple Rock, which is exactly what you are supposed to do. But the thrashing current naturally pulls you into the rock, so avoiding it takes lots of effort.

In the aftermath of the activity, we reviewed a videotape of our day's activities and discovered that those rafts that avoided the rock had one thing in common, and you can guess what it was—all the people in the raft were rowing in the same direction.

Upon further analysis, there was one other key element that led to success. The rafts that made it safely by the rock had leaders (raft captains) who were clearly communicating instructions to the rowers. The rafts that hit the rock lacked that clear communication, and the rowers in those rafts were each left to decide for themselves what to do.

We learned that day in the raft that both leadership and followership are of equal importance. An organization (be it a business, a nonprofit, or a family) without leadership and without a clear communication of vision, direction, and expectations will surely hit some of the rocks in the river. So will an organization where the members of that organization are not united with their leaders and are each going in their own direction. It takes everyone working together on the raft to make the journey a safe one.

This has some clear implications for every organization that merits a few questions: First, if you are the leader, have you clearly communicated the vision, strategy, and direction of the company to the team members? Does everyone know the role they play and how to accomplish it? Second, as a team member, do you understand the vision and the direction that has been developed, and are you willing to do your part? It is only when everyone is consistently rowing in the same direction that success is achieved.

Climb on board your raft, grab an oar, lead, or follow, and row in the same direction. Enjoy the ride.

Invitation to Act

Take time to assess your organization and your role and determine what you can do to get everyone on board and in sync.

What are your thoughts, feelings, and impressions?

24

The Difference Is YOU

We live in a world of almost limitless choices. The average consumer can choose between multiple providers of nearly every product and service imaginable. And whether you are a student selling tickets to a school play, a Girl Scout selling cookies, a local business owner selling a product or service, or an employee of a nonprofit trying to raise funds for a worthy cause, what you are really selling is YOU. YOU make the difference.

Now please don't get me wrong, your product or service is important. You can't provide a second-rate service or a poor product. But at the end of the day, people choose to do business with YOU.

Think about all the places where you choose to do business—your hair stylist, the restaurants you frequent, the place where you buy your car (or the place where you have it repaired), and the stores where you grocery shop, buy your appliances, purchase your clothing, and do your local gift shopping.

In almost every case, if you are honest, someone (or many someones) who work there are a key motivation for you to do business there.

We once had a microwave oven die on us, and we decided to replace it. Off we went to do our shopping. But did we shop multiple stores? No. We went to a local furniture/appliance store because we know the people who own the store—and we trust them. They are honest and fun to do business with, and we know they care about us.

Could I have found the microwave cheaper somewhere else? Perhaps. But the thought never crossed our minds simply because of the relationship we have with the person who owns the store and the salesperson who takes care of us. We knew they would go the extra mile to make our experience a satisfying one, and we didn't think about going anywhere else.

Here's another example. One of our bank employees was contacted by a man who owned a business far outside of our normal market area. Our employee used to provide banking services to the owner while employed at another bank. The owner wanted to move his entire banking relationship to our organization, even though we were almost thirty miles away. Why?

The answer is simple—he valued his relationship with our employee. His choice to move all his loans, deposits, and other banking services was not based primarily on the products and services we provided. It was based on a relationship.

Wherever you do business, for the most part, you do so because there is someone you trust or like who works there. It may be their kindness, their punctuality, their attentiveness, their enthusiasm, their professionalism, their creativity, their humility, their honesty, their generosity, their follow-up, their smile, their sense of humor, their wit, or their wisdom. But in the end, it is people who make the difference—for good or for bad.

The question then is this: What do people think of YOU? Are you the reason people choose to affiliate with your organization, or are you the reason they don't? Sometimes a brutally honest look in the mirror reveals opportunities to eliminate the blemishes in life that limit our success.

I recommend taking the time to list all the reasons you do business where you do. Make a list of the virtues that inspire you to shop where you shop. Ask yourself what it is about the people there that you really admire. Then ask yourself if you are providing the same inspiration to those who shop or associate with you. Sometimes (painfully so) product development needs to be replaced with "Me Development."

Harry Beckwith, author of the book *What Clients Love*, has a page in the book that reads as follows:

What the Best Salespeople Sell (in order)
Themselves.
Their company.
Their service or product.
Their Price.
Sell yourself first.

If you want to be successful in selling your products or services, sell YOU—the very best YOU.

Invitation to Act

Take an honest look at YOU. What changes do you need to make in the way you work and serve to sell the very best YOU?

What are your thoughts, feelings, and impressions?

25

Service with a Smile

There is an old Chinese proverb that says, "The pleasure of doing good is the only one that will not wear out." How true that is. Nothing lifts your spirit quite like helping someone else and nothing seems to leave a longer, lingering feeling of satisfaction.

January and February in the Midwest can often seem like long, gloomy months with lots of dark, cloudy days. Some people head to Florida or Hawaii, to the tanning booths, or to the spa, and others find their way to the movies or an excellent restaurant.

But given the quote about doing good, combined with the fact that many around you may be feeling the blues, no matter what month we are in, one prescription for a sunnier day is to make a concerted effort to do good for someone else. Smile at them, make them laugh, offer them a cookie, write them a note, make an unexpected phone call to say "thank you," or tell them a good joke.

Our youngest daughter is a wonderful example of this principle. Since her infancy we have called her "Merry Sunshine," as she always seems to have a smile on her face. And she radiates that sunshine to others. Her positive, cheery attitude, good humor, and desire to serve others has helped her excel as she has interacted with team members in volunteer and work environments.

Such behavior brightens the lives of the receiver and brings deep feelings of satisfaction and enjoyment into the life of the giver. And such acts are simply good business. It is so good, in fact, that doing good is the subject of many business books, one of which is *The Fred Factor* by Mark Sanborn.

I quote now from the inside jacket of the book: "Mark Sanborn recounts the true story of Fred, the mail carrier who passionately loves his job and who genuinely cares about the people he serves . . . Where others might see delivering mail as monotonous drudgery, Fred sees an opportunity to make a difference in the lives of those he serves."

The book recounts story after story of people (like Fred) who seem to embrace the attitude that is well summarized in the following quote: "I expect to pass through this world but once, therefore any good that I can do, or any kindness that I can show to any fellow creature, let me do it now; let me not defer it or neglect it, for I shall not come this way again." (Stephen Grellett, 1773–1855)

We all know intuitively that this is true. Yet in the busy pace of everyday life, doing good for others often takes a back seat to the demanding schedule of meetings and events, and we find ourselves passing through time without making a real difference.

I go back to today's prescription. Try filling it, taking the first dose, and making someone's day. In the end, the smile that comes across their face may be just the ray of sunshine you need to chase away the dark clouds.

Invitation to Act

Decide today to do something to lift another. It can be done for a friend or a stranger. Go make someone smile.

What are your thoughts, feelings, and impressions?

26

No More "What-Ifs"

What if I had made that investment? What if I had not sold our home? What if I had started saving when I was younger? What if I had apologized? What if I had started my diet earlier? What if I had sunk that last putt? What if? What if? What if?

The fact is we've all made some mistakes. There have been missed opportunities, bad decisions, and we've choked at a critical moment. Life is full of these events and always will be. The key is to learn from them, fix them to the best of our ability, and not look back. Too much time is wasted in reliving our mistakes, instead of improving our future.

A few years ago, I missed an important meeting. Somehow it just never made it into my planner. I felt so bad and remember sitting in the living room berating myself for having made such a foolish blunder. I finally went on with the day but continued to languish over what I had done.

At one point my wife (who knew of my error) noticed that I seemed to be down and asked me what was wrong. I told her that I kept thinking about the mistake I had made and how disappointed I was for having made it.

She responded with a question: "So what will you do about it?"

I told her that I had already made a firm resolve not to make the same mistake again. Again, her response was a question: "So don't you think you've learned your lesson and that you can stop punishing yourself?" I smiled, got up, and went on my way determined to stop asking myself, "What if?"

The truth of the matter is that life is short. We can spend our days pining over the what-ifs in life, or we can refocus our energy on the what-wills of life. For example, you may not have started saving money until later in life. Accordingly, you may be tempted to ask yourself the question, "What if I had started saving when I was twenty?"

True, you could calculate how much you would have saved—but what good would that do? The real question—the more important one—is this: "What will you do about it now that you know it's a problem?" Face it, nobody can remake yesterday's putt on the eighteenth hole. But we can practice for tomorrow's putts.

Healthy hearts and minds learn from the past, apply the lessons today, and plan. Progress requires pro-activity, not paralysis. And while the what-wills lead us to action, the what-ifs freeze us in our tracks.

Take one last look at your collection of what-ifs and drop them into the circular file. Then stand up, step forward, and start moving with a life filled with exciting what-wills.

Invitation to Act

Pick an area of your life where you keep going back to a what-if and replace it with a what-will. Let go of the past you can't change and move forward with what you can do.

What are your thoughts, feelings, and impressions?

27

From Lemons to Lemonade

Summertime in Michigan is filled with endless days of enjoying the beaches, the weather, the fresh fruits and vegetables, and the pure delight of summer vacation.

Among the fondest of my summer memories is watching children set up the traditional neighborhood lemonade stands. With unbridled enthusiasm and dreams of making a fortune, they sit for hours, enjoying the magic of turning something sour into something salable.

It is a simple wonder that you can turn something so sour into something so sweet. And though there is rarely any wealth accumulated, the children store up priceless memories while basking in the summer sun and enjoying the richness of life.

Such is one of the great lessons of life in summertime—that from lemons comes lemonade. Life is full of ups and downs, twists and turns, and its share of lemons, and no one is exempt from them. Lemons come in the form of economic, mental, physical, professional, emotional, and interpersonal setbacks and challenges. They are not limited to age, gender, or race, and only one thing is certain about lemons: they will come. Our only choice is what we will do with them.

Lemons, in and of themselves, are very sour and leave a powerful pucker in their wake. It is only when we add the element of sugar that lemons begin their magical conversion into a satisfying summer beverage.

Life is a lot like that. As the lemons of life present themselves, sometimes one at a time and sometimes in whole bowls, we must choose if we will pucker up and sip the sour, or if we will add a bit of sweetness to the mixture and enjoy a singular treat.

Such was the case with a man by the name of Karoly Takacs. Takacs was a member of the Hungarian pistol shooting team and was quite good. But in 1938, while serving as a sergeant in the army, a defective grenade exploded in his right hand—his shooting hand—permanently damaging the hand beyond use. After a lengthy stay in the hospital, Takacs went into seclusion to train with his other hand. The following year he won the Hungarian pistol shooting championship, and in 1948, he won a gold medal in the Olympics in London.

It would have been easy for Takacs to suck on the lemon of self-pity, but he did not. Instead, he pulled out the bags of sugar labeled "good attitude" and "perseverance" and began adding cups of sweetness to the bowl of lemons. For him, the lemons turned into Olympic gold.

Sometimes someone else can add the sugar to the bowl of lemons for us. Then, if we will only drink, we can enjoy the sweetness brought to us by others.

One boyhood summer, our parents made the decision to remodel our home. This meant moving into a small apartment above a bank in a city about fifteen miles from where we lived.

Under those circumstances, our lives were disrupted and unsettled, and we bathed in water that smelled like rotten eggs. We had no furniture, except for foldable lawn chairs, and we no longer had access to the lake, the yard, and the friends that we had anticipated enjoying over summer vacation. Summer, we were certain, was full of sour gulps.

But somehow, in the close quarters of that summer retreat, Mom and Dad made magic. They introduced us to comic books and the local drugstore, which offered candy and a soda fountain. We took long walks through town and played games at night on a small card table. And we added bubble bath in large doses to the bath water.

The interesting thing to me is that of all my boyhood memories, some of the sweetest emerged from that bowl of lemons above a bank. I will forever be grateful to my parents for teaching us how to mix a little sugar and water with the lemons we encounter on our journey through mortality.

Whatever your circumstances, whatever your age, and wherever you are in life, take the time and make the effort to make some lemonade when lemons come your way. You might even help someone else do the same. Your reward will be the sublime satisfaction of turning painful puckers into sweet smiles.

Invitation to Act

Look for an opportunity to turn a lemon in your life—or in the life of someone else—into lemonade.

What are your thoughts, feelings, and impressions?

28

The Devil's in the Details

How many times have you looked at something superficially, only to wish later that you had examined it thoroughly? Whether it is buying something, checking on a child's homework, or managing an employee, the devil is always in the details.

Simply stated, the details of a situation almost always reveal the truth of the situation, including the problems. I once knew of a salesperson who kept telling his boss that "everything is going great." For months, the sales lagged, but the salesperson insisted that things were about to turn around.

Finally, the boss sat down with the salesperson to review a list of very specific questions such as, "How many contracts do you have that have been signed?" "How many sales calls have you made?" "How many orders are in process of being filled?"

Well, you can probably guess what the answers were—no contracts, no calls, no orders. Once again, the devil really was in the details and usually is.

Generalities, like large dark clouds, hide the facts in the shadows. It is not until we shine the light on the details that the truth comes forth.

Why do people tend to avoid the details? First, it takes work. Sorting through the details requires time, effort, and discipline. It requires rolling up the sleeves and diving into layers beneath the surface. It is rarely convenient and can be very time consuming. In short, it is not easy.

Second, there are times when we are all afraid of finding the truth. We would rather enjoy blissful ignorance than deal with the realities of the situation. The car looks good, so we buy it without a detailed inspection. The homework appears to be done, so we acknowledge it without examining the answers. The employee appears to be working hard, so we don't monitor performance. The contract appears to be simple, so we don't read it before signing.

Third, those around us may not want us to dig into the details as it may lead to the truth being discovered. Even the Wizard of Oz did his best to discourage Dorothy from digging too deeply into the facts of the situation. Remember his words: "Pay no attention to that man behind the curtain." Well, she did, and she got to the truth, painful as it was.

I think Harvey S. Firestone summed it up best with these words, "Success is the sum of details." Day by day, as we examine detail by detail, we ultimately see things the way they really are. By lifting the fog of generalities and letting the light of details reveal the true facts, we obtain better information, make better decisions, and find greater success.

Invitation to Act

The next time you are tempted to respond superficially to information provided to you, dig for the details. Ask questions, gather information, kick the tires thoroughly. Then, once you have done your homework, act on the information you have acquired.

What are your thoughts, feelings, and impressions?

29

Check Your Compass

I grew up racing sailboats with my dad. The most exhilarating races were held on Lake Michigan where the wind and waves often created challenging circumstances. Every race was an adventure, and some of my fondest memories come from times with Dad out on the boat.

Over the years, we won many races, due principally to the skills and disciplines my dad developed as the skipper of his boat. One of those disciplines that remains a valuable lesson to me was his determination to constantly check the compass.

In sailboat races, the boats travel toward floating buoys placed miles away from the starting point of the race. The only way to reach the buoy is to follow the compass heading that is given to each skipper at the start of the race. With the effects of the wind and waves, the boat is often pushed off-course, requiring regular directional corrections if the skipper wants to reach the buoy and win the race.

To this day I can remember Dad calling out to me to check the compass affixed to the boat and call out the heading so he could adjust the direction of our boat.

Life is a lot like the boat races that we used to enjoy. Each of us journeys toward lofty goals in life—be they economic, educational, physical, or spiritual. But sometimes we forget to pause and check our compass to make sure we are staying on-course and moving in the right direction. Then, as stated by the Pulitzer Prize–winning American poet, W. S. Merwin, "We are asleep with compasses in our hands."

A compass is a device that tells us where we are headed. It is a unit of measurement. If checked consistently, it gives assurance that we are making progress toward our destination.

In pursuing our life's goals, it is important that we have compasses and that we use them. Measuring life's compasses can be as simple as paying attention to your feelings as you move down a path, or as structured as setting up specific, measurable criteria for evaluating your progress. The compass for a dieter can be a scale, while the compass for a business owner may be a survey of customer and employee satisfaction, combined with a careful review of financial results. For success to be achieved it is important that you have a compass and that you use it.

No matter where you are headed in the race of life, be like a successful skipper: grab your compass, check it often, and win the race.

Invitation to Act

Pick any goal you are pursuing in life and determine whether you have identified the compass to use to monitor your progress—and whether you are using it. If not, begin to do so. Check it often and it will help lead you to the achievement of your goal.

What are your thoughts, feelings, and impressions?

30

Go Make Some Mistakes

We all have a few traits in common, and one of them is the fact that we make mistakes. Some mistakes, like cobwebs in a closet, remain hidden from the world and are known by few. Others seem to shine like the noonday sun for the entire world to see. Some are trivial while others are consequential.

Mistakes can destroy us, or they can propel us to new heights. Most generally, the choice is ours. So, in celebration of (or at least in tolerance of) mistakes, here are a few thoughts on how to make the best of them:

- **Don't be afraid of making them.** Albert Einstein put it this way, "A person who never made a mistake never tried anything new." Fear leads to paralysis. When we fear making a mistake, we stop trying. Then our progress comes to a halt.

- **Learn from them.** In the end, mistakes are one of our greatest teachers. In fact, if you look back on your life, you will discover that most of your deep and important learning came from the mistakes you made. James Joyce said, "A man's errors are his portals of discovery." Take the time to examine your mistakes and to extract the golden nuggets of knowledge and experience that they offer.

- **Admit them and, where possible, fix them.** Confucius taught his students, "A man who has committed a mistake and doesn't correct it, is committing another mistake." Some mistakes simply can't be remedied or undone. But where they can be, the benefits are significant. As hard as it is, admitting and fixing mistakes is as important to our learning as making them.

- **Laugh at them.** Take the time to find the humor in life, even in the worst of your mistakes. Laughter lightens our burdens and helps us keep a healthy perspective on life.

Remember, in the words of Edward Phelps, "The man who makes no mistakes does not usually make anything."

Invitation to Act

The next time you make a mistake—and there will be a next time—admit it, do your best to fix it, find the humor in it, and write down what you learned from the experience.

What are your thoughts, feelings, and impressions?

31

Energize Through Exercise

This chapter is going to both hurt and help. It is an invitation to jump-start your day and your life by jumping, or running, or walking, or whatever you choose to do to get your heart beating, your muscles working, and your body moving.

Now I know that many of you, like me, might be tempted to adopt the sentiments of a quote attributed to both Mark Twain and Robert M. Hutchins who said, "Whenever I feel like exercise, I lie down until the feeling passes." But before you stop reading and set this aside, please fight the temptation and read on.

According to the Mayo Clinic and the Centers for Disease Control, regular exercise has many benefits. Among them are better weight control, reduced risk of heart disease, strokes, and diabetes, and the development of healthy bones, muscles, and joints.

And in addition to these important elements, most experts agree that exercise energizes. It promotes feelings of well-being and reduces stress. It gives a sense of victory over self. In short, it puts spring in your step and optimism in your attitude.

I won't make any recommendations regarding the type, frequency, or level of exercise that is best for you. You can obtain that information from a multitude of reliable sources. And if you have not exercised in the past, a discussion with your physician should precede any commitment to action.

As busy as life gets, exercise is one of the easiest important tasks to put off. Some might even consider it distasteful. Charles Schulz once said, "Exercise is a dirty word. Every time I hear it, I wash my mouth out with chocolate."

But my own personal experience has proven otherwise. Some years ago I began to run, starting out with what seemed to be an impossible one-mile adventure. Before I knew it, I was up to five miles, then almost fifteen miles. Ultimately, I ran a full marathon in Washington, DC.

What I discovered in the process were the wonderful changes that occurred as I consistently exercised. I lost a few pounds, my clothes fit better, I slept more soundly, and I began to feel energized.

Politician Joan Welsh was once quoted as saying, "A man's [or woman's] health can be judged by which he [she] takes two at a time—pills or stairs." So, whatever you do to exercise, do something. And energize through exercise.

Invitation to Act

Put together a plan to exercise on a regular basis, however modest it is. Then execute on that plan and enjoy the results—or a candy bar.

What are your thoughts, feelings, and impressions?

32

First Impressions

Like it or not, the old saying that you only get one chance for a first impression is true. Whether it is a first date, a public debate, an effort to sell a product at someone's doorstep, or the first time a customer enters your place of business, you get one shot at a first impression. And, for better or for worse, first impressions do last.

Whether you observe or present a sloppy appearance, poor service, improper grammar, dirty windows, or an indifferent attitude, a bad first impression can taint the rest of the experience by setting low expectations.

If the windows are dirty in a restaurant, we might expect the plates, silverware, and bathrooms to be the same—and we don't go in. If the store clerk is rude, we may expect the products to be faulty. If the first view of a guest speaker reveals stains on a tie, we may end up looking for flaws in the speech. And the list goes on. Just think of how many times you have experienced a first impression that left you determined never to have a second encounter.

I knew of a family who had come to visit a small Midwestern community for the first time, having heard positive comments about the stores and entertainment available there. The family shopped for a while, then entered one of the restaurants for a bite to eat. There they found the service to be so slow, and the server to be so rude, that they left the restaurant, and the town, with a resolve that they would never return. They even took the time to contact a local community leader to share the story and reiterate the fact that they would never visit the town again. While the decision was shortsighted, it illustrates the powerful effect that first impressions can leave.

The reality is that we live in a world of almost unlimited options. We can buy what we want, wherever we want to, and most people won't settle for something less than remarkable.

Truly, positive first impressions are powerful persuaders. A positive first impression sets our heart and mind on a journey of searching for the best in others and helps us find patience when subsequent experiences are not up to par. But a negative first impression does just the opposite.

Go ahead, take a good look in the mirror. Check your teeth, comb your hair, use good grammar, provide exceptional service, wash the windows, polish the furniture—and make a great first impression. It may be the only one you will ever have the chance to make.

Invitation to Act

The next time you have an opportunity to leave a first impression, take the time to ensure that it is a remarkable one. Think through what you will wear, say, and do to make your first impression a great one.

What are your thoughts, feelings, and impressions?

33

What's Your Message?

Every day we communicate with those around us. Some of that communication comes in the form of words. Most of it does not. Of all the communication we engage in, the old axiom is true: our actions speak louder than our words.

What we do daily comes from who we are. For the most part, nice people do nice things. Kind people do kind things. Caring people do caring things. And the opposite is also true. Our actions spring from our heart and they communicate the truth about who we are.

That is why Gandhi was quoted as saying, "My life is my message." He understood that what he did conveyed who he was. And his actions were consistent with his words.

Fortunately, we can choose to change what we do, often resulting in a change in who we are. Hands that once stole, and now serve, can lead to a heart that once was hard and is now softened.

A fair question for each of us then is this one: based on the way I am living, what message am I sending to those around me?

This question has application in almost every aspect of our lives. No matter who we are or what role we play, our actions are sending messages. I once had a boss who was very demanding and set extremely lofty standards. But that same boss never allowed me to leave his presence without first spending time inquiring about how each member of my family was doing. He never told me that he was a family-oriented person or that he cared about me—he simply showed it, and I worked hard for him because of it.

The truth is, everything we do or don't do, sends a message. And what's the implication of that fact? It is simply this: if you want to teach an important principle, truth, or behavior to someone else, live that principle, truth, or behavior. Be the message you want to convey. If you want to teach courtesy, be courteous. If you want to teach service, serve. If you want to teach discipline, perseverance, or the benefits of exercise, then add doing to your speaking, let your example be the greatest teacher, and let your actions speak louder than your words. In the end, the greatest teachers are those who walk their talk.

Life flies by so quickly and each waking hour is a precious opportunity to send important messages to those around us. What is your message? I wish you well as you ponder it and deliver it by what you say and do.

Invitation to Act

Examine your daily behavior and ask yourself what you are teaching through that behavior. Your actions will teach more than your words.

What are your thoughts, feelings, and impressions?

34

Meaningful Meetings

We all have too many meetings to attend, most of them last far too long, and many of them are significantly less effective than they could be. In the words of John Kenneth Galbraith, "Meetings are indispensable when you don't want to do anything." Accordingly, here are a few ideas that may turn meaning*less* meetings into meaning*ful* meetings.

The most basic rule to follow in deciding whether to meet or not is to remember that it is better not to meet than to waste time. If you can't make it beyond this rule, then cancel the meeting—or don't schedule it in the first place.

There are many reasons to hold a meeting, whether face-to-face or virtual. These include communicating information, sharing ideas, evaluating data, making decisions, or brainstorming. The most powerful meetings are those where intellect is utilized and energy is created, not extinguished.

In that regard, it is fair to ask yourself whether you could accomplish the same thing by sending an email, making some phone calls, or posting some information on a website. If your objectives can be accomplished without meeting, then resist the temptation to do so. In this realm of life, less is usually better.

If you are going to meet, consider these suggestions for enhancing the quality of your meeting. They are simple, commonsense ideas that may help you get more done in less time with fewer complaints.

- **Suggestion 1:** Few meetings should last more than one hour. While there are exceptions to every rule, if you are well prepared, an hour should be sufficient time to get the job done. In addition, the attendees of every meeting should have a clear expectation of the start and finish time of the meeting.

- **Suggestion 2:** Set a definable, measurable objective for every meeting. Participants should know this in advance, so they can mentally prepare themselves for the work that lies ahead. This is a matter of both courtesy and effectiveness.

- **Suggestion 3:** Materials to be read should be distributed, read, and pondered in advance of the meeting. Failure to do so leaves everyone scrambling to get up to speed during the meeting, leaving less time to discuss the material and make meaningful decisions.

- **Suggestion 4:** Stick to the agenda. You called the meeting for a reason so make sure you stay on track with that plan. Meandering from subject to subject is best done elsewhere.

- **Suggestion 5:** Finally, always take minutes. They hold participants accountable for decisions that are made and serve as documentation for meaningful follow-up. Even simple, concise minutes are better than no minutes at all.

Applying the discipline of a few simple suggestions to our meetings can reduce their quantity and increase their quality.

Invitation to Act

Evaluate the most recent meeting you held and determine, based on these suggestions, what you would have done differently. Prior to scheduling your next meeting, review these suggestions and decide how to move forward.

What are your thoughts, feelings, and impressions?

35

The Bigness of Little Things

Some time ago I had lunch with a man who took his children—and one granddaughter—on a cruise. At one of the sumptuous dinners the little granddaughter had eaten far too much and was very sad that she was too full to enjoy one of the decadent desserts that had been prepared.

When the waiter came to the little girl and asked what dessert she would like, she got a sad look on her face, lowered her head, and said, "Nothing." With that, the waiter left with the rest of the orders—then quickly returned with all the goodies.

After serving the other guests at the table, the waiter walked up to the little girl and placed before her a beautiful plate stacked high with whipped cream. And drizzled across the whipped cream was the word *Nothing*, written in Hershey's chocolate syrup. Everyone at the table, especially the little girl, was delighted with the wonderful bigness of this little thing.

The truth is, taking care of the little things reflects the bigness of our hearts. Little things take time and effort and are almost always intimate and personal. They demonstrate care and concern and show that we are in tune with the needs of those around us. And they are often unexpected, which adds to the magic of the moment.

Little things characterize great organizations and great people. Whether it is your favorite restaurant, store, friend, or event, the likelihood is that the little things they do are a big part of why they are your favorite.

While I was living out of the country for a few years just after college, my beloved dog, Duke, became ill back home, and the veterinarian told my parents that his days were numbered. Mom wanted to write and tell me but knew that he would be gone by the time her letter arrived.

When the letter did arrive at my apartment, it was addressed to me, but to my surprise, the return address read, "Your Best Friend." As I opened the letter, my eyes fell upon these words, "Dear Rick, By the time you receive this letter, I will no longer be here on earth, so I wanted to share with you some of my happiest memories of our time together."

In essence, Mom had written the letter for my dog, highlighting the memories that we enjoyed together over the twelve years of his life. The letter was signed, "Your Pal, Duke."

I still have that letter, written by a mom who took the time to do a little thing that made such a big difference in my life. It turned a sad event into a sacred one and remains one of the great treasures that I possess.

Whether you are a parent, a child, a sibling, an employer, an employee, an associate, a board member, or a friend, take the time to make a big difference by doing a little thing.

Invitation to Act

Think of someone you know and determine what little thing you can do for them that will make a big difference in their life.

What are your thoughts, feelings, and impressions?

36

Adjust!

Few things in life are as certain as the predictability that change will occur. Accidents happen, economies falter, illnesses strike, wars are declared, and tragedies occur. That is simply part of life. It always has been, and it always will be. The only variables in this regard are what the changes will be and when they will occur.

But there is another variable of inestimable importance that has nothing to do with how or when change occurs. That variable is how each of us responds to change when it arrives. My wife, Dyana, has a favorite word that she uses when talking about unexpected changes. That word is *Adjust!* Note the exclamation point. In Dyana's mind, this is not a passive explanation. Rather, it is a proactive declaration.

You may have seen the "No Whining Allowed Here" signs that find their way into homes and workplaces. The word *Adjust!* in our home is a lot like that sign. It is a clarion call to stop worrying and start working. Sure, each of us has the right to mourn over an unfavorable shift of the winds in our lives, but like the famous country-western singer Dolly Parton once said, "We cannot direct the wind, but we can adjust the sails."

The truth is, the faster we Adjust! the happier we will be. Life can become quite dreary if we allow ourselves to live in a self-constructed prison of sorrow and self-pity.

In 1982, Mark Inglis lost both legs in a mountain climbing accident. But in 2006, he became the first double-amputee to summit Mt. Everest. He Adjusted! In 1981, at the age of thirteen, Erik Weihenmayer lost his eyesight due to a disease called retinoschisis. Twenty years later, in the year 2001, he became the first blind climber to summit Mt. Everest. He, too, Adjusted!

Adjusting is not always easy, and it is okay to mourn the loss of the circumstances or plans you had in place. That is only natural. But after an appropriate time of languishing over what we lost, the time will come to Adjust! and move on.

Change is certain; how we deal with it is not. It is all a matter of choice. Whatever life doles out, Adjust! No matter what happens, use your ability to choose your attitude, your behavior, and your vision for the future. No matter how dark the clouds of life may seem, the sun will rise tomorrow, and you will have another day in which to learn, to grow, and to experience the beauty in the world around you.

Invitation to Act

The next time your life or plans are unexpectedly altered, Adjust! Explore your alternatives and identify your options. Then choose to focus on what you can do, not on what you can't do.

What are your thoughts, feelings, and impressions?

37

Kindle Your Curiosity

One of the remarkably enjoyable things about being a father of six children is witnessing the unbridled curiosity that guides them along on the journey of discovery. At infancy, their eyes are wide open, and they explore the magical details of every facet of life. Then, when speech enters the scene, life becomes an unbroken series of questions regarding everything, everybody, everywhere.

Rudyard Kipling summed it up well with these poetic words: "I keep six honest serving-men, They taught me all I knew; Their names are What and Why and When and How and Where and Who."

Curiosity is the cradle for creativity and the door to discovery. It transforms the ordinary into the extraordinary and lights the fuse that ignites endless explosions of knowledge, invention, and opportunity. This was evidenced so clearly in the life of Albert Einstein, who said, "I have no special talents. I am only passionately curious."

The truth of the matter is that curiosity is at the heart of all real learning. It allows us to see things that we normally would not see and learn the things that would otherwise elude us. This was attested to by Bernard Baruch, with this profound observation: "Millions saw the apple fall, but Newton asked why."

My invitation to you is to dive back into the pond of curiosity and start splashing in the waters of wonder. Take a walk and ask questions about everything you see. Why *is* the sky blue? Where and what is the kingdom of Tonga? How do birds communicate with each other? Ask people about their life, their career, their ideas, and their opinions. Read a book about some subject with which you are unfamiliar. Search the internet for answers to literally any question you might have. (Did you know that bees can't fly in the dark? Have you ever wondered how toothpicks are made?) Open your eyes and find the magic in the moment.

Now a warning: curiosity requires humility. We can only be curious when we acknowledge the fact that there is so much we don't know. Children ask so many questions because they have no fear of their ignorance. They simply don't care what we think about their questions; they just want answers. Their quest for knowledge is not stifled by the poison of pride. And the more they know, the more they want to know.

To those who think curiosity killed the cat. Well, Arnold Edinborough offers an appropriate response with this insightful quote: "Curiosity is the very basis of education and if you tell me that curiosity killed the cat, I say only the cat died nobly."

Your first assignment: go find out who Arnold Edinborough was and why he felt that way, find out if cats really do have nine lives. Kindle your curiosity.

Invitation to Act

Ask questions about everything. Be curious about the people, circumstances, and world around you. Pick a topic you are interested in and explore it.

What are your thoughts, feelings, and impressions?

38

Exercise Your Agency

According to the dictionary, *agency* is the capacity to act or exert power to accomplish something. An insurance agent acts as an agent for the insurance company and has the power or agency to sell the company's product. A real estate agent has the agency to act on behalf of someone buying or selling a home. Likewise, each of us has agency to act for ourselves. We are free to choose—every hour of every day—how we will use our agency.

My experience is that the greatest growth and the greatest rewards come to those who exercise their agency without being asked or told to do so. And this is true whether we are nine years old or ninety-nine.

A child who chooses to clean their room without being asked to will be the recipient of appreciation and recognition—and will feel good about doing it. So will the employee who chooses, of their own free will, to voluntarily take on a tough task, or to deliver more than was expected. Truly, the road to riches is traveled by people who use their agency to do good and to accomplish much.

Far too often in life we wait to be told what to do and, in so doing, we miss opportunities to grow, to achieve, and to lift others' burdens. As Henry Ford once put it, "You can't build a reputation on what you're going to do." In other words, reputations are built on what is *done*, not on what one intends to do. And the best way to build a life, a career, and a reputation is by exercising our agency to do something we see needs to be done.

But exercising agency does not come without a price. It requires choosing our actions wisely and pursuing our course even in the face of opposition.

Exercising agency to do something good is the equivalent of building your own harbor for your ship to come in. It can be likened to constructing your own door for opportunity to knock. It is the key to your own treasure box—whatever the treasure you are seeking may be.

Daniel E. "Rudy" Ruettiger is a notable example of this principle. As a young man whose dream was to play for the Notre Dame football team, Ruettiger did not wait to be invited. He approached the team and was given an opportunity to play on the Notre Dame scout team, which is a practice team that scrimmages with the varsity team to help them prepare for games. In that capacity he constantly did more than what was expected, sustaining multiple injuries and setbacks.

His determination to exercise agency to do good won him the right to play for one game on the Notre Dame varsity team. And in his one play of a lifetime, he successfully sacked the opposing quarterback and was carried off the field on the shoulders of his teammates. Agency exercised for good almost always leads to superior results.

Don't wait to be told what to do—just do it. Find a need and fill it. Do more than what is expected. Look around, identify a void, and act. Don't wait, don't hesitate, just do it without being told.

As the 1913 Nobel laureate for literature, Rabindranath Tagore stated, "You can't cross a sea by merely staring into the water." A sea of opportunity awaits you, so dive in and start exercising your agency to do good. And enjoy the good that comes your way.

Invitation to Act

The next time you see an opportunity to make a difference, to do good, act without being asked to. Just do it of your own free will.

What are your thoughts, feelings, and impressions?

39

What's in a Name?

Of all the words we may hear during the day, few are as endearing and heartwarming as our own name. The Scottish poet Thomas Campbell put it this way: "Who hath not own'd, with rapture-smitten frame, the power of grace, the magic of a name."

What's in a name? Just about everything. It is given at birth and remains until death. Some names elicit emotions of profound respect. Others are a reminder of less-desired characteristics and attributes. Our life is spent building the meaning and reputation behind our name, and our tombstone will memorialize it for those who follow us.

Hearing your name can raise you to the heights of joy and exhilaration or send you spiraling to despair. For example, your name, as announced at your graduation, your wedding, your promotion, or your arrival home from a long journey, brings joy, excitement, and happiness. But hearing your name taken in vain, spoken of unkindly, or used disparagingly, brings sorrow and disappointment. And so does the lack of use of your name.

I once worked with someone whom we all addressed by name. But in all the years that I worked with him I don't ever remember him calling me by name. I was not offended, but I missed the extra warmth that the use of a name can bring into a friendship.

Awhile back, I was speaking to a group of elderly residents at a retirement facility. One of them introduced herself to me and said that, though her name was Ella Mary, most people just called her Mary—and she did not like that. "My name is Ella Mary," she said, "and I wish they would call me that."

Later that day I gave a presentation to this wonderful group and afterward was packing up to leave when I saw Ella Mary about to walk out the door. I walked over to her and gently held her hand and said, "It was a pleasure to meet you, Ella Mary." She responded with warmth that melted me and said, as she squeezed my hand, "Thank you for remembering my name."

A few days later I had occasion to speak at another retirement facility to a group of ten residents. As they walked into the room, I took the time to memorize their names. When the time came for me to speak, I began by welcoming them and then pointed to each one and said, "This is Fred, this is Sarah, this is Melanie, this is Robert..." until I had named each one. When I said the last name, the room erupted into a round of applause. Names really are important.

Each day, for better or for worse, we build our name. Someday, it will be used by others as a symbol for what is good, or for what is not. The choice is ours.

Likewise, each day we can brighten lives, warm hearts, and spread joy as we take the time to remember—and to use—each other's names in a way that promotes kindness and friendship.

Invitation to Act

Learn, memorize, and use the names of others. And live worthy of your name.

What are your thoughts, feelings, and impressions?

40

Follow Through

Whether you are throwing a baseball, shooting a basketball, swinging a golf club, or taking a stroke with a tennis racket, one of the inevitable keys to success is the follow-through. Allowing your hands to follow through in any of these activities adds accuracy and energy to the shot. In fact, watch a coach offering counsel to nearly any athlete and you're bound to hear the words, "You need to follow through."

Following through is as critical to success in life as it is in sports. People who follow through earn the trust and respect of those around them. They can be counted on to get the job done, and they demonstrate a maturity that opens the doors to additional opportunity.

While working in banking, I was called on by two sales representatives, each representing competing companies that sold a service that was of interest to us. Each salesperson did an impressive job presenting their company and the service they could provide, and both had a compelling story to tell. But when it came to following through, one salesperson stood out.

Rather than waiting a few days to send a follow-up letter to me, this salesperson sent me an email the next morning, summarizing the conversation we had and confirming the agreed-upon next steps. His willingness to follow through so quickly and effectively won him the upper hand in the contest for our business.

Follow-through does not take a lot of time or money. It does take a lot of discipline—self-discipline, that is. But in the end, the price that is paid for consistently following through yields a return on investment that is enviable by any measure.

Each of us already knows whether we are good at following through, and where we need to improve. The challenge is to decide today—now—that from this point on we will follow through with the commitments we make and with the activities we know will lead to increased success.

No matter who you are, where you are, or what you are doing in life, make follow-through a priority in your pursuit of excellence. Do what you say you will do, do it promptly, and do it well. You will find that your achievements in life, and your satisfaction with life, will increase as your follow-through improves.

Invitation to Act

Look for an opportunity to follow through in any endeavor, large or small. Do it in a way that sets you apart from others.

What are your thoughts, feelings, and impressions?

41

Look Up

In today's world we are often bombarded by news and views of devastation that occurs throughout the world. Sometimes, just listening to these reports can really bring us down. When this happens, our tendency is to look for the negative, rather than the positive, in everything around us. But before succumbing to the downward pulls in life, consider the following:

First, Stephen Covey, the author of the book, *The 7 Habits of Highly Effective People*, teaches a wonderful principle. He explains that in life we all have concerns regarding the world around us: wars, natural disasters, or the price of gas, for example. This constitutes our large Circle of Concern. But he reminds us that within the Circle of Concern there are things over which we have *no* control, and there are things over which we *do* have control. The things over which we *do* have control fall into a smaller circle called our Circle of Influence.

Covey's counsel is to focus our thoughts, our actions, and our energy on the things that fall within our Circle of Influence—the things we can control. Now let me give you an example.

You and I may be concerned about the price of gasoline. But we have no control over the price of gasoline. It is within our Circle of Concern but outside our Circle of Influence. Thus, although we could spend hours of time worrying, talking about, and being depressed about the price of gasoline, none of these endeavors will change the price of gasoline.

We do have control, however, of where we buy our gasoline and how we use it. These decisions *are* within our Circle of Influence. We can look for gas stations that offer lower prices. We can come up with shorter routes to do daily tasks. We can line up all our random errands throughout the day or week into one (or a few) well-planned trips. We can keep our tires inflated to obtain more miles per gallon. We can arrange for carpools to work, church, school, or other activities. And the list goes on.

There is much we can do within our Circle of Influence. And the fact is, the happiest, most productive people spend little time worrying about things they cannot change and spend lots of time thinking about, planning for, and doing what they can change.

Second, life is often a matter of keeping proper focus and perspective. Imagine, for example, that there was once a young boy whose parents took him to see the vast beauty of Niagara Falls. Just as they arrived at the falls, the boy spilled some chocolate milk on the top of his brand-new white tennis shoes, and he could not take his eyes off the terrible stain. Everywhere the family walked, they basked in the incredible beauty of the falls, but the young boy did not. He ended up leaving the falls without ever really seeing them, having never taken his eyes, or his thoughts, off the stain on his shoes.

The lesson in this story is simple: you must raise your sights above the negative events in life and take the time to see the beauty.

I once had a vivid reminder of the importance of lifting our eyes to see the beauty that is around us. As I was preparing to head off to work, I surprised our eight-year-old son by telling him that I would take him to school. Normally I left before he did in the morning, but on that day, I left later to be with him.

Prior to leaving the house, I had listened to the news, and it was filled with a litany of worrisome events. I was clearly preoccupied with the effects the news might have on our lives. Yet, as my son and I rode merrily along to school, it occurred to me that he was as happy as happy could be. We laughed, and talked, and teased, and as we arrived at school, he bounded off, skipping down the sidewalk with a smile that went from ear to ear. He had been with his dad, and it didn't matter that the world was a bit in shambles.

My heart was full, and I arrived to work a happy man, determined to focus more of my time on things within my Circle of Influence and to spend more time looking up and around at the good and beautiful things that surround us.

Spend your time and energy on things you have control over (your Circle of Influence) and take the time to lift your eyes off the dirty tennis shoes and look up. Doing so can turn the blues into the beautifuls and will lead to increased effectiveness, personal productivity, and happiness.

Invitation to Act

As you go through the next couple of days, allow yourself to focus only on changing things you have control over, and don't spend time thinking or worrying about the things you can't control. Likewise, take a few minutes each day and just reflect on the good and beautiful things that surround you, no matter what is going on in the world around you.

What are your thoughts, feelings, and impressions?

42

Hurry Up by Slowing Down

When was the last time you asked yourself (or anyone) the question, "When is life going to slow down?" If you are like most people, it is a question that is asked with increasing frequency and rising frustration. And fast food, cell phones, social media, and unlimited internet exploration only hasten the speed at which life is flying by.

For the most part, we are overbooked and underwater; we are drowning in an ocean of endless agendas, information, and options. And it will only get worse. The changing technological landscape will put more information at our fingertips, and society will increase the expectations for personal performance.

But hastened pace does not always lead to heightened productivity. In fact, in most cases, the adage "haste makes waste" proves itself to be abundantly true. What can be done to assist us in slowing from warp speed to the mere speed of light?

Here are a few suggestions that may help.

- Schedule time for yourself in your daily planner by labeling it "meetings with myself" or "time for really important things." So often we end up accepting invitations to meetings or events simply because there was a blank space in our calendar. Filling in some of those blank spaces with time for yourself will give you an excuse to say no to other invitations and will allow you to use the time to recharge, refresh, and revitalize.

- Develop the new habit of allowing yourself plenty of time to get to the next appointment. Leave a little early so your ride (or walk) can be relaxed, and your mind can be calm and clear. Trying to speed through town to make up for having left late for a meeting creates stress and replaces peace with panic. Leave a little early and enjoy the ride.

- When entering a conversation, communicate up front how much time you have available. Failure to do so keeps you more focused on the clock than on the conversation. If you must run off somewhere in ten minutes, state that up front. Then you won't have to worry about deciding when and how to explain that you must cut the conversation short. It also assists the person with whom you are speaking to be concise in their conversation.

- Learn to say no. It's one of the hardest things to do in life but also one of the most important. You have only twenty-four hours a day just like everyone else. And those hours are precious commodities. Before saying yes to any invitation, ask yourself who you will be robbing time from to accept it. Then ask yourself if it is worth it. And remember, you need time for yourself. Trying to do everything for everybody can leave you as the one victim from whom all time is robbed.

- Take time to ponder. Schedule some early morning time every day to read, ponder, and reflect on life. Count your blessings. Plan your day. Reflect on your values and priorities. This constitutes warming up before getting on the daily treadmill of life.

- Make time to relax and to play. Take a long shower. Soak in a hot bath. Grab an ice cream cone in the middle of the day. Read a book. Listen to your favorite music. Author a poem. Take a walk with someone you love.

Life will not slow down, but we can. Amid all the changes and choices in life, a little effort to hurry up by slowing down will allow us to be more productive and to smell an occasional rose along the way.

Invitation to Act

Pick any one of the recommendations in this chapter and apply it today. Once you discover how it edifies your life, consider picking another one and trying it. Take your time and enjoy the activity.

What are your thoughts, feelings, and impressions?

43

Preventing Procrastination

Of all the behaviors that rob us of time, peace, and happiness, few are as universally experienced as that of procrastination. According to the dictionary, to procrastinate is "to put off intentionally the doing of something that should be done." Simply stated, it is avoiding doing something less pleasurable so that something more enjoyable can be done. It is trading the mundane for the marvelous, the boring for the beautiful, or the routine for the exciting.

The problem is, the boring, the mundane, and the routine are frequently the must-dos in life, while the marvelous, beautiful, and exciting activities are often the want-to-dos. Unfortunately, when we begin to trade the essentials for the electives, we run into problems. Classes are failed, jobs are lost, relationships are damaged, progress is halted, and frustration abounds. Alyce Cornyn-Selby sized it up well with the words, "Procrastination is the grave in which opportunity is buried."

In the spirit of putting an end to procrastination, here are a few suggestions:

- Stop overcommitting. So much of procrastination comes from accepting too many invitations (out of a sense of obligation) to do things we don't have time to do. Think twice, maybe three times, before saying yes.

- Break the big elephant projects into manageable bites. We often avoid a task because the start-to-finish time seems unbearably long. Converting the one big task into many little tasks can take the distaste out of diving into our duties.

- Mix the must-dos with the want-to-dos throughout the day. Don't set an unrealistic goal of tackling all the tough jobs all at once. Keep balance in your budget of time.

- Plan a reward for yourself for completing one of those onerous tasks. It doesn't have to be a big reward, but give yourself a pat on the back for stepping up to the plate.

According to a Spanish proverb, "Tomorrow is often the busiest day of the week." By choosing to do *today* the things that should be done today, we can reduce chaos, lower our blood pressure, and avoid the negative consequences that procrastination brings.

The next time you are tempted to put off a task until one of these days, remember, in the words attributed to both Henri Tubach and H. G. Bohn: "One of these days is none of these days."

Invitation to Act

Stop procrastinating today. Decide now that it's time to learn and apply correct principles and leave this habit behind.

What are your thoughts, feelings, and impressions?

44

Step Outside the Box

The phrase "thinking outside the box" represents one of the most ubiquitous notions of our day. Many books have been written on the subject, and the phrase is used in almost any setting or meeting where creative thinking is needed.

The origin of the phrase may not fully be known, but according to Martin Kihn of *Fast Company*, it has something to do with a puzzle used by consultants in the 1970s and 1980s. The puzzle is called the Nine Dots Puzzle and appeared as early as 1914 in Sam Loyd's *Cyclopedia of 5000 Puzzles*.

The object of this puzzle, shown below, is to connect the nine dots using only four straight, connected lines, without ever lifting the pencil from the paper. Go ahead and try it. Then turn the page to see the answer. But here is one hint. To solve the puzzle, you must think (and draw) outside of the box. You must go outside the boundaries that your mind sees. And that is what thinking outside of the box is all about.

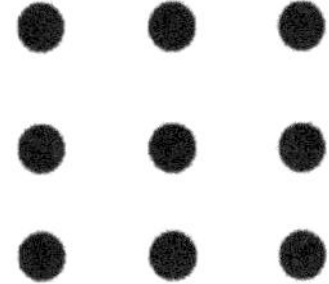

It was Albert Einstein who said, "We can't solve problems by using the same kind of thinking we used when we created them." This implies applying different thought processes (different from those we've used in the past) to solve the problems we now face. But to *think* outside of the box it truly does help to *step* outside of our boxes.

Stepping outside of our boxes is best done by getting out of our offices. Some years ago, we wanted to focus on improved service at our bank. The normal thing to do would have been to visit other banks or hire experienced bank consultants. But that would not have taken us outside our banking box.

Instead, we took a group of our employees to go shopping at a mall. Each employee visited a number of the notable retailers in the country, ranging from clothing stores to electronics stores and from perfumeries to restaurants. With each visit we took copious notes regarding what we saw, heard, smelled, felt, and experienced. The results were wonderful—and led to the discovery of ideas and solutions that made a profound difference for good in what we did.

Perhaps this quote from a Special Report in the June 12, 2007, online edition of *Business Week* magazine will best illustrate the importance of stepping outside of your box:

> The Frisbee. The escalator. Reinforced concrete. These vastly different inventions share one thing in common: They weren't invented exactly—each was borrowed from an unrelated field. The flying toy was inspired by the metal pie tins of the Frisbie Baking Company that college students of yore tossed for fun. The escalator was originally conceived as a Coney Island amusement ride. And reinforced concrete was first patented in 1848 by a French gardener trying to develop a better flowerpot.

Remember that whatever it is that you are trying to develop, solve, invent, or create, think outside of the box by stepping outside of the box. By the way, here's the solution to the puzzle.

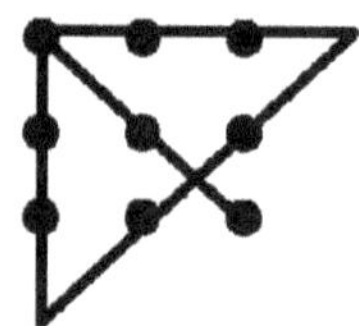

Invitation to Act

The next time you encounter an obstacle or an opportunity that needs to be addressed, think outside of the box. Reach out to others for ideas. Go tour other businesses or organizations. Read publications from other industries or have lunch with someone in an unrelated field. Think outside of the box by stepping outside of your box.

What are your thoughts, feelings, and impressions?

45

Create Your Own Playing Field

Most of us, particularly those involved in sports or business, have heard someone refer to the desire for a level playing field. This terminology refers to any situation in which competitors have an equal advantage and must adhere to the same rules and where no one has an unfair competitive advantage.

If the playing field is not level, and one competitor has an unfair advantage, it is in the best interest of the disadvantaged competitor to fix it—to level it. After all, who would want to compete when the odds are already—and unfairly—stacked against you?

This is true whether you are dealing with a high school football team that allows ineligible players to play, or with a business that uses unethical practices to obtain information about their competitors. Unlevel playing fields are not fair, and the competitors have a right to try to level them.

But as good as it is to level the playing field, it is even better to create your own playing field. In life, we often tend to compete on someone else's terms—on their playing field, rather than creating one of our own.

I experienced this a few years ago when invited to represent the bank I worked for at a local business exposition. Each company was asked to set up a booth that told the company's story. As I began to do some research, I learned that most of my competitors had large, beautiful booths costing more than $20,000 to build. Our booth was really nothing more than an inexpensive foldable stand that rested on top of a table.

After assessing the situation, I decided we needed to build a bigger booth, like our competitors, and we started down that path—until it hit me. By building a bigger booth we were doing nothing more than competing on someone else's playing field (the big booth playing field), instead of focusing on creating a unique playing field of our own. So, we dropped our plans for a big booth and headed down a different path—that of creating a playing field that would be fun and unique.

To create our own playing field, we pulled together a group of employees from nearly every department of our bank. They brainstormed and came up with an idea that put us on the scoreboard in a significant way.

Rather than using a booth, our employees recommended that we utilize a team of employees dressed as referees in the customary black-and-white-striped shirts, with tennis shoes, and a whistle around the neck. And in place of a table full of displays, we had a miniature basketball court.

Each guest walking by was invited to take a few shots at the hoop. And with each shot made, the referees blew their whistles, and the guest received a ticket to put into a drawing for an all-expenses-paid cruise for two. It was fun, engaging, and inviting, and we always had a crowd at our booth. The total cost was a tenth of what we would have spent on the booth, and the results were many times better than what a booth would have brought us.

The following words offered by Henry Ford emphasize the importance of continually creating your own playing field: "The competitor to be feared is one who never bothers about you at all, but goes on making his own business better all the time. Businesses that grow by development and improvement do not die. But when a business ceases to be creative, when it believes it has reached perfection and needs to do nothing but produce—no improvement, no development—it is done."

Such is the case in life. When we worry too much about others' playing fields, we miss the opportunity to create our own. Then inspiration is often replaced with desperation, which leads to frustration. I invite you to go beyond leveling the playing field. Instead, create your own playing field—and win.

Invitation to Act

When looking for opportunities to set yourself apart in any field of endeavor, don't try to level the playing field – create your own.

What are your thoughts, feelings, and impressions?

46

Gratitude

In today's busy world, one of the least heard but most needed phrases consists of just two simple words—*thank you*. Those two words can lift spirits, soften hearts, heal wounds, and inspire lives. Saying thank you is one of the courtesies in life that costs nothing but is truly priceless.

It almost goes without saying that people who express gratitude are more enjoyable to spend time with, and they seem to enjoy life more. Truly, as stated anonymously, "Gratitude is the best attitude."

Cicero, the great Roman orator, once said, "A thankful heart is the parent of all virtues." Thus, cultivating gratitude in our lives leads to a powerful posterity of attributes and characteristics that will enrich us and those around us. In fact, those who are truly grateful tend to be those who are kind, caring, and prone to serve others. Just stop to reflect on the people in your life whom you admire the most, and there is little doubt that gratitude will be at the heart of the virtues you cherish most in them.

Yet, in the pace of life, expressions of gratitude are often abandoned—not out of malice—but out of a sense of expediency. We are sometimes so busy that we simply find it difficult to replace convenience with courtesy. We all need to make a concerted effort to become grateful and to express gratitude.

Such was the case with Shannon Broom, a young lady who lost her life in a tragic automobile accident on May 1, 1998. Following her death, her parents discovered a Gratitude Journal that Shannon had kept for almost a year. The journal contained a daily record of five things she was thankful for each day. It included the simple, everyday things in her life that made her happy.

I suspect that Shannon's daily, silent expressions of gratitude served to enhance her appreciation of all that was around her—and led her to say thank you for the kindnesses extended to her. The more grateful you are, the more grateful you become. And once you begin to recognize the big things in life for which you feel gratitude, your heart becomes tuned to recognize the smaller things as well.

Feeling gratitude should lead to expressing gratitude. In a world filled with skepticism and criticism, a simple thank-you has endless potential to make a difference for good. And in life, you tend to get what you give. Those who thank others become the recipients of thanksgiving themselves.

Plan to be grateful. Keep your own journal of gratitude. Stop to reflect on those kindnesses, large and small, for which gratitude should be felt and expressed—then express it. Say thank you to those around you.

Thank the mail carrier, the grocery clerk, the bank teller, the Uber driver, the receptionist, the repair person, and the customer service associate. Thank your children, your parents, your spouse or significant other, and your friends. Say thank you to anyone and everyone for anything and for everything. Be grateful. Express your attitude of gratitude.

Invitation to Act

Thank someone today for something. Don't wait until tomorrow. Then do it again tomorrow, and the next day, until it becomes a habit.

What are your thoughts, feelings, and impressions?

47

When Was the Last Time You Were a Hero?

In life, some questions are easily answered and are soon forgotten. Others cause us to look deeply within ourselves and seem to echo in our hearts for an extended period. Such may be the case with the question posed in this chapter: When was the last time you were a hero?

Heroes abound around us. Some are well known with names that span history. Others are scarcely recognized. Such is the case with Arland D. Williams Jr.

On January 13, 1982, Williams was a passenger aboard the ill-fated Air Florida Flight 90 that took off in freezing conditions from Washington National Airport. The flight had been in the air for only a few moments when it lost altitude and crashed into the 19th Street Bridge spanning the Potomac River. The plane then plummeted through the ice-covered river, killing seventy-three of the seventy-nine passengers upon impact. The remaining six passengers quickly swam to the icy surface where they continued their battle for life.

A few moments later, a park helicopter arrived and lowered a rescue cable to Williams. But instead of placing the safety strap around himself, Williams handed it to woman floating nearby. She was carefully lifted to safety, after which the helicopter returned two more times to Williams.

Each time, however, Williams refused to save himself. Instead, he handed the safety line to the remaining passengers, whose lives were spared. When the helicopter finally came back to rescue Williams, he was gone. He had silently slipped away, having given his life for people he didn't know.

There is little question that Arland D. Williams Jr. is a hero. He is an inspiration and a reminder of what we all can aspire to be—heroes to those in need.

And while we hope that none of us will be asked to give our life for another, we can all give of our life*style* for others. That sacrifice can come in a variety of forms.

For example, you might consider making a financial donation to a local charity or two. Even a few dollars a month can make a significant difference, and most charities can arrange for a direct deduction from your payroll check. Your willingness to give up a few extras in life may be the means for providing someone with some precious necessities.

Likewise, you can volunteer at any number of local nonprofit organizations. The employees at these entities would gladly welcome a helping hand. You can read to the sick, help build a house, offer to serve on a board of directors, or assist with a fundraising event. The options are endless.

Finally, don't forget that heroes are often most needed right in your own backyard. Taking the time to help a child with a project or sharing a listening ear with a family member can qualify you, in their eyes, for hero status.

Arland D. Williams Jr. gave his life. What are we willing to give? Each of us has the capacity to give up something, to make some sacrifice, and to become a hero to the men, women, and children in our lives who need heroes every day.

Invitation to Act

Set some time aside today to consider how you can be a hero to someone.

What are your thoughts, feelings, and impressions?

48

Remember

Few words in the English language have a more powerful effect on our heart and mind than the word *remember*. In our earliest years we are counseled to remember to wash our hands before we eat, to get our chores done, and to remember any number of instructions or words of advice designed to guide and protect us. Remembering in this context really does help keep us out of trouble.

As we grow older, symbols around us begin to help us remember the things that are most important to us. For example, the flag of a nation helps its citizens to remember their heritage, traditions, and pledges of loyalty and allegiance. A wedding ring likewise helps us remember the vows made between a husband and a wife. Even the appearance of the team mascot on the basketball court or football field can be a symbol that causes team members to remember who they represent, and to battle with greater vigor in pursuit of victory.

As we move into the golden years of life, it is our ability to remember that allows us, in the words of James M. Barrie, "To have roses in December." Indeed, it is the memory of loved ones now departed, of happy times spent in days gone by, and of the lines and chapters in the book of our lives, which allow us to remember and relive, repeatedly, the treasured moments of mortality. William Maxwell said it well, "I have liked remembering almost as much as I have liked living."

How can remembering make a difference in our personal and professional lives? The answers are as endless as the challenges each of us might face. But one thing is for certain: remembering can focus us on the things that matter most.

Whether it's a promise we made, a lesson we learned, a truth we treasure, a memory we have cherished, or a goal we have set, remembering can calm us, comfort us, inspire us, direct us, warn us, and propel us to greater achievement and more satisfaction in life.

In that regard, you may remember the Disney movie, *The Lion King*. In the movie, a young lion cub named Simba suffers the death of his father, the Lion King Mufasa. Mistakenly believing that he had contributed to his father's death, Simba sinks into sorrow and abandons his right to the throne.

Later, in a poignant scene, Simba sees an image of his father in the clouds—which then speaks to Simba these words: "Simba, you have forgotten who you are . . . You are more than what you have become. Remember who you are . . . Remember."

This call to remember stirred up the best in Simba, who was reminded of his heritage, his duty, and his destiny. Simba then, having been focused and fortified by remembering, goes on to take his father's place in fulfilling his destiny as the Lion King.

The truth of the matter is that each of us, like Simba, needs to take the time (and occasionally be reminded) to remember. Whether in a Disney movie, or in real life, all of life's greatest lessons are only of value to the extent that we remember them.

In our daily, constant effort to move forward through life, let's take time to look back and remember the things that matter most. In doing so we will find the strength, the courage, and the wisdom required to make our journey both joyful and successful.

Invitation to Act

When confronted with either opportunity or adversity, take time to remember. Remember your heritage, your dreams, your past lessons in life, your relationships, and your potential.

What are your thoughts, feelings, and impressions?

49

Plant the Seeds, Pull the Weeds

In our backyard we have a modest garden, replete with fruits, vegetables, and herbs enjoyed by our family. And each year, sometime in the middle of the summer, I pause to reflect on the principal activities that govern success in the world of gardening—planting seeds and pulling weeds.

It is abundantly evident that without the planting of seeds, there could be no harvest. Every bean, pea, tomato, or strawberry began as a seed and grew from there. And the law of the harvest reigns eternally true. What you sow is what you reap. Corn comes from corn seeds and wheat from wheat seeds. It's a formula that simply doesn't change.

Pulling weeds is the second main activity that determines both the quantity and the quality of the outcome of a garden. And it seems that from the moment a seed is planted, weeds spring up magically and menacingly, seeking to rob the seeds of the life-giving moisture and nutrients needed to grow and flourish. Left unattended, weeds multiply and intertwine with the young seedlings, making the extraction of the weeds both difficult and dangerous.

Life is a lot like a garden. We are constantly given opportunities to plant seeds and pull weeds. The more we plant, the greater the harvest. And the more diligent we are at pulling the weeds, the more abundant our harvest will be. Which leads to the questions: What more should I be planting? What weeds yet need to be pulled?

I once read a fictional story about a man who was asked by a friend if the man would like to quadruple his income. The man enthusiastically responded with a definite "yes," and asked his friend to tell him how he could accomplish this. The friend responded by telling the man that it is a remarkably simple formula that consists of two activities.

"First," he said, "start doing everything you know you should be doing. Second," he added, "stop doing everything you know you should not be doing."

Or, in other words, start planting seeds and start pulling weeds. Each of us has an ample supply of seeds to plant—seeds of kindness, seeds of patience, seeds of hard work, seeds of charity, seeds of success. Plant them, and, given the law of the harvest, they will grow.

Likewise, each of us has an abundance of weeds in our garden. Weeds of idleness, weeds of selfishness, weeds of impatience, weeds of failure. Pull the weeds and our seeds will flourish.

Life is a lot like a garden. An empty plot of land can become a tantalizing tapestry of fruits and vegetables. It all boils down to planting seeds and pulling weeds. So, go plant and pull and enjoy the harvest.

Invitation to Act

Take an honest look at yourself. You know what you need to start doing and you know what you need to stop doing. Pick one thing to start and one thing to stop and watch the seeds grow.

What are your thoughts, feelings, and impressions?

50

The Best Medicine

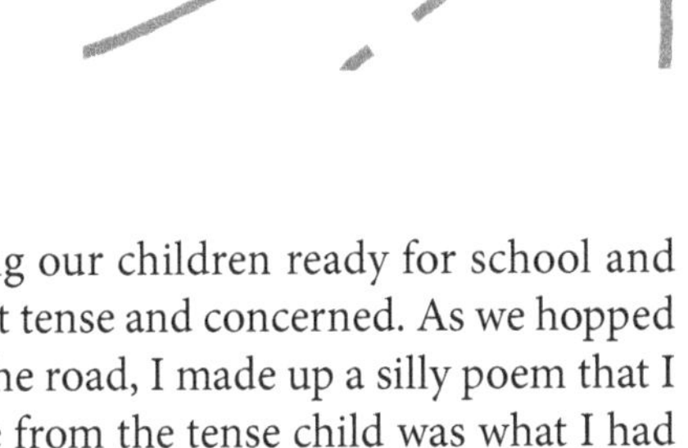

The other day we were getting our children ready for school and one of them seemed to be a bit tense and concerned. As we hopped in the car and headed down the road, I made up a silly poem that I recited to them. The response from the tense child was what I had hoped for—first a small smirk, then a smile, and then a healthy, gentle laugh. From that moment on, things were fine, and the tenseness was replaced with a relaxed, contented demeanor.

The old saying about laughter being the best medicine does have some truth to it. In fact, gelotology is the study of laughter and humor and the many psychological and physiological effects humor has on the human body. Laughter has been linked to improvement in heart conditions, diabetes, blood flow, immune responses, and sleep and anxiety disorders.

Psychologist Steve Sultanoff, PhD, who served as the president of the American Association for Therapeutic Humor, is quoted as saying, "With deep, heartfelt laughter, it appears that serum cortisol, which is a hormone that is secreted when we're under stress, is decreased. So, when you're having a stress reaction, if you laugh, apparently the cortisol that has been released during the stress reaction is reduced." That alone is reason enough to go read a few good joke books.

Laughter is also fun. It turns gloom into glee and lightens heavy moods. Something funny adds sunshine to dark days and puts a smile on everyone's face. It is also a way of disarming volatile, emotion-packed situations and of connecting people. Victor Borge once said, "Laughter is the shortest distance between two people." In a world with endless languages, dialects, and conflicts, laughter is a universal language that connects heart to heart and conveys warmth and openness.

Likewise, laughter can be a refreshing break from the pace of our intense schedules, as Milton Berle noted when he said, "Laughter is an instant vacation." It really is. When we laugh, we are quickly removed from our worries and can enjoy a moment of refreshment.

Given the benefits of laughing, we should all do it more often—and help others do the same. Take time to learn some good jokes and share them. Look for the humor in situations and use that good humor to improve the quality of your interactions. Learn to laugh at yourself. Sometimes we take life so seriously that we deny ourselves the healthy chuckles that make life a little easier to navigate.

An old Yiddish proverb had it right: "What soap is to the body, laughter is to the soul." Go lather up, head to toe, and enjoy the cleansing, purifying, healthy effects of laughter. And share some of those suds with those around you.

Invitation to Act

Decide today to make healthy humor part of your repertoire. Learn a few good jokes, laugh with a friend, and bring smiles to others.

What are your thoughts, feelings, and impressions?

51

Be the Solution

Sydney J. Harris, a noted American journalist, was once quoted as saying, "If you're not part of the solution, you're part of the problem." I echo Harris's sentiment and invite you to consider being the type of person who does more than identify what needs to be fixed.

How many times has someone approached you with a complaint, a concern, a criticism, or a problem, only to walk away leaving you holding it all in your hands? Don't get me wrong, identifying problems *is* important—critically important. But the real benefit comes when meaningful alternatives for solving the problem are shared.

Some time ago, someone in our bank was asked to share some public remarks about a difficult situation but was given very little information about the situation. The employee recognized that he lacked adequate information and could have gone to his boss with a legitimate concern. But, instead, the employee took the initiative to do some research and gather the information he needed to make appropriate remarks. He then went to his boss with both the problem *and* the solution. And the value of his personal stock rose significantly.

In a world where time is precious and challenges are limitless, a high premium is paid for those who can be the solution to the problems they identify. Whether at home, at school, at church, or at work, every organization has problems that need to be fixed, and they never have enough time or resources to solve them.

So be the solution. Put on your thinking cap before you serve up a problem or a complaint. Develop a list of solutions and a recommendation that is as compelling as the problem itself. Then serve the solution with the problem and watch the smiles—and the relief—appear on the face of the recipient.

Henry Ford sized it up quite succinctly with this quote: "Don't find fault. Find a remedy." Be creative. Be innovative. Take the time to think. And be the solution.

Invitation to Act

The next time you come across a problem or a challenge, don't complain, don't whine, don't go to someone else for answers. Be the solution by finding some solutions and making some recommendations.

What are your thoughts, feelings, and impressions?

52

Face Your Fears

Spiders. Heights. Public speaking. Failure. Success. Enclosed spaces. Needles. Mice. Going to the dentist. The dark. The list of things that instill fear in us is as diverse as each of us.

Some fear is healthy. For example, the fear of being hit by a car while crossing a busy street causes us to be alert and attentive before moving our feet. But in many cases fear can be paralyzing, creating problems in our day-to-day living.

As one unknown author articulated, "Fear of monsters attracts monsters." Thus, someone who "freezes" due to fear, while crossing the street, may bring about the very incident they feared.

Please don't get me wrong. This chapter is not an invitation to ignore fear or to discount its role in protecting us. After all, the fear of jumping into shark-infested waters with nothing on but a bathing suit is probably a healthy fear that will lengthen your life. Nor is this an invitation to be careless or less than prudent in assessing risk. Rather, this is an invitation to face your fears and to move forward in life. Facing our fears means determining the true nature of them, then deciding how we can move ahead in life despite them.

So often we choose not to engage in activities that could lead to personal progress and success, simply because we fear them. This is particularly true in pursuits such as public speaking, dating, joining athletic teams, taking on new work assignments, changing jobs, and choosing a host of other alternatives in life.

One of ours sons was afraid of heights, roller coaster rides, and anything that looked dangerous. So, you can imagine how startled we were when we received a call from him while at high school, announcing that he had decided to join the diving team. His friends had encouraged him, believing he would be successful. He evaluated the opportunity, looked fear in the face, and decided to go for it. And he became a very good diver despite his fears.

Regarding fear, Ralph Waldo Emerson said, "Fear defeats more people than any other one thing in the world." Why? Because our mind can create scenarios far more disastrous than reality. Then we cower at the presence of an enemy who, in many cases, is only a phantom of our own imagination. An old Swedish proverb sums it up nicely: "Worry gives a small thing a big shadow."

To face a fear, we must assess the true risk, seek to mitigate it the best we can, then decide to move ahead despite it—or not. The true risk of public speaking, for example, is embarrassment, not death. How can we mitigate that risk? Preparation and practice are two viable answers.

Eleanor Roosevelt offered wise counsel for those who are fearful of taking the plunge: "You gain strength, courage and confidence by every experience in which you really stop to look fear in the face. You are able to say to yourself, 'I have lived through this horror. I can take the next thing that comes along.' You must do the thing you think you cannot do."

Invitation to Act

The next time you are hesitant to do something that could be of great value, because of fear, take time to understand it, to determine the true risk, and to reduce the risk as best you can. Then face your fear and forge ahead.

What are your thoughts, feelings, and impressions?

53

Collaborate

This chapter is a celebration of collaboration. It is an acknowledgment of the veracity of that old saying, "Two heads are better than one." According to the dictionary, to collaborate is to work jointly with others, especially in an intellectual endeavor.

Collaboration requires cooperation and imagination. And it requires humility—a willingness to admit that you alone do not have all the answers. Woodrow Wilson, twenty-eighth president of the United States, exemplified collaboration. As the architect of legislation that led to the formation of the Federal Trade Commission and the Federal Reserve System, he was once quoted as saying, "I not only use all of the brains I have, but all I can borrow."

Every day, all around the world, more is getting done with less through the efforts of collaboration. Small businesses join together to purchase bulk items on a discount basis. Scientists from multiple countries share research and resources in the battle for a cure for cancer, vaccine for viruses, and treatments for life-threatening illnesses. Churches of differing denominations collaborate to address common social challenges. And the list goes on.

How does one go about collaborating? That's easy. First, find any problem that you, your family, church, business, nonprofit organization, or community is struggling with. Then find someone with a similar concern and begin a dialogue. That first step may lead to a journey filled with opportunities and solutions.

I knew a man who saw a need to clean up his community. The growing presence of litter, graffiti, and a lack of beauty led to a dialogue with a few other community members. This led to brainstorming about ways to improve the situation.

The small group invited the chamber of commerce, the local newspaper, and some business owners to become part of the collaborative effort. Ideas were generated, funds were raised, and an event was created.

Now, in that community, an annual spring cleanup day involves anywhere from 1,000 to 3,000 people. Litter is gathered, graffiti is eliminated, flowers are planted, and the city shines.

Collaboration starts with people who care, and flourishes as people communicate. It arises out of trials, challenges, and the desire to create opportunity, and it often culminates in remarkable accomplishments.

Whatever your status in life may be, and whatever challenges you may face, pick your problem, or identify your opportunity, then don't hesitate, collaborate.

Invitation to Act

Identify one challenge or opportunity that you, or an organization to which you belong, is facing. Pull together a group of people facing similar challenges and collaborate. Share ideas, create solutions, share the joy of success.

What are your thoughts, feelings, and impressions?

54

Save Your Bullets

Imagine a deer hunter going out in search of the prized 16-point buck. He has a limited number of bullets and a goal of securing some prize trophy. As he is walking through the forest, he sees a large number of small animals such as rabbits and squirrels, and he begins to shoot. One by one he takes his small prizes and continues to press forward.

Suddenly, and unexpectedly, he finds himself face-to-face with a record size buck, larger than he has ever seen. Thrilled at his opportunity he raises his rifle, looks into the scope, and takes aim. He pulls the trigger and hears a soft click, but the gun does not fire. In his relentless pursuit of the smaller animals, he has spent all his ammunition. The bullets are gone.

Sometimes in life, as it pertains to our relationships with others, we are like the big game hunter. Critical comments, even constructively critical comments, are like bullets. And we often waste our supply of them on things that don't matter much, only to find ourselves out of ammunition when something significant needs to be addressed. William James said it well with these words: "The art of being wise is the art of knowing what to overlook."

The fact is, in any relationship, there are only so many bullets you can fire. This is true in manager-employee relationships, husband-wife (or significant other) relationships, and parent-child relationships.

In fact, recent research shows that for a healthy relationship to exist there should be at least five positive comments made for every negative or critical comment that is uttered. With children, an 8 to 1 ratio is even better. And when that ratio declines to just one positive comment for every one negative comment, the relationship becomes dysfunctional. Imagine what it would be like in a situation where there are five negative comments for every positive comment—truly destructive.

The fact is that after hearing constant criticism, people eventually shut down. Then, when something important needs to be addressed, there are no bullets left. And even if there were, they would have no meaningful impact.

What does this mean for each of us? At the very least, it calls for a careful evaluation of how we communicate with each other. Try keeping track of the number of positive messages you say to someone—compared to the critical comments you make. Then adjust accordingly. Maintaining a healthy ratio of positive to negative comments takes effort. But most important things in life do.

The time may come when you need to discuss a life-changing or life-threatening issue with a son or a daughter. Or you may need to address a serious situation with an employee, a work associate, or a friend. When that situation occurs, you will be grateful to have a little extra ammunition.

Whether out in the fields and forests, or in the warm, cozy comfort of your living room, always remember to use your ammunition sparingly and save your bullets.

Invitation to Act

Begin to keep track of the positive versus negative comments you make in just one relationship. And the next time you anticipate making a negative thought, ask yourself if it is worth spending the bullet.

What are your thoughts, feelings, and impressions?

55

An Ode to Optimism

In a world that is often skeptical, cynical, and pessimistic, I offer an Ode to Optimism, seasoned with a touch of realism.

Says the Pessimist . . .
> It can't, it won't, I doubt it will
> Something goes wrong, I know.
> A failure is what it will be,
> And surely time will show,
> That all we do and all we try
> Is destined but to fail.
> So, let's give up and give up hope
> And tell our sorry tale.

Says the Optimist . . .
> It can, it will, we'll make it so
> It will work if we do too.
> Success is ours, you can bet on that
> We won't quit till we are through.
> And all we do and all we try
> Will lead us to our quest.
> So, let's get up and go to work
> And do our very best.

As this ode illustrates, the same thing can be viewed and esteemed differently by different people. It is all a matter of perspective. Said Sir Winston Churchill, "A pessimist sees the difficulty in every opportunity; an optimist sees the opportunity in every difficulty." When pessimists see a hole in the ground that needs to be filled, optimists see a swimming pool. Thus, optimism is also aided by vision and creativity.

Truly, optimism consists of viewing the world around us with faith, hope, and enthusiasm for the future. The fruit of optimism, even when faced with failure, is hope and happiness.

But even optimism sometimes deserves a tender touch of reality. Thus, as stated by William Arthur Ward, "The pessimist complains about the wind; the optimist expects it to change; the realist adjusts the sails."

One thing is always true. We can choose how we think. Both pessimism and optimism are conscious choices that lead to varying paths and consequences. And both pessimism and optimism can become habit forming. Thus, it does take effort to replace pessimistic lenses with an optimistic prescription. But the effort is worth it. Optimism leads to growth and the hope of a new season, as echoed by Susan J. Bissonette, who said, "An optimist is the human personification of spring."

Invitation to Act

Decide now, today, to think differently, as you look differently at the world around you. Look for opportunity in adversity. Apply creativity to calamity. Be optimistic. And let the winters of life bloom roses of spring in all you say and do.

What are your thoughts, feelings, and impressions?

56

Don't Agonize, Organize

It's midnight and you're lying in bed, wide awake. Your head is spinning because you have too much to do and too little time in which to do it. You have deadlines, duties, and demands for your time, and on top of it all, you can't find your car keys or the bill you were supposed to pay.

Sound familiar? If you are like most people, you've been there, done that, and may be still doing it. How do you fix it? By applying the words found in the quote by Florynce Kennedy, from which the title to this chapter was derived, "Don't agonize. Organize." Accordingly, here are some basic ideas for organizing your way to survival and success:

- Get the floating phantoms out of your head and onto paper. Keeping your to-do list in your head leads to clutter and confusion. Sit down each day, preferably at the end of each day or early in the morning (when your mind is fresh) and write down the list of everything that is swimming around in your head. This will free up some of the space in your brain to be concerned with how-to-dos rather than with what-to-dos. There are also a multitude of software applications available for your smartphone, smart pad, laptop, and other devices onto which you can enter and prioritize your to-dos.

- Establish habits for dealing with the routine (but important) functions in your life. For example, when you come into the house, have a set place to put your keys, your cell phone, purse, and other items. Developing habits for the mundane but critical functions of your life will eliminate some of the frustrations that rob you of peace, creativity, and fun.

- Develop forms or checklists to use in managing your life. Before a pilot takes off in a commercial airliner, there are required checklists to follow. This ensures that no function or activity, whether big or small, is missed. It forces the pilot to think through the entire trip before it ever begins and prevents problems from occurring. Likewise, each of us has daily, weekly, and monthly responsibilities that require some careful consideration and proper planning. Creating and reviewing a checklist of the important tasks to think about or do on a regular basis is a discipline that can save us time and energy and help us focus on things that matter most.

- Set up systems for dealing with paperwork. Where do you put the bills when you receive them? When do you pay them? How do you keep track of your finances? Where do you store your vital records and important documents? By setting up simple systems to keep track of these items and perform these tasks, you avoid a multitude of problems that otherwise could arise.

The reality is, organization takes time, but it saves more. It is an investment in the present that yields dividends down the road. It is a pathway to increased personal peace and power. So get out your pen and paper, put on your thinking cap and don't agonize—organize.

Invitation to Act

Take some time to examine and evaluate how you are organized. Look for opportunities to create systems for your day-to-day functions that are easy to follow and maintain.

What are your thoughts, feelings, and impressions?

57

Painless Public Speaking?

Few things in life are feared as much as public speaking. Even the mere thought of it can cause strong knees to quiver and steady voices to shake. It can lead to lightheadedness, nausea, and panic attacks and is often avoided as if it were a pestilent plague.

Nevertheless, few of us, at least at some point in our lives, can avoid having to speak in public. Thus, we ought to make it as enjoyable as possible—or at least as painless as possible.

In the spirit of reducing pain and increasing enjoyment, I offer these tips for your public speaking moments in life:

- Do your homework. If asked to speak about something, spend whatever time is necessary to learn about that subject. Nothing brings more confidence than knowing you know the facts about the topic on which you are speaking. The greater your depth of knowledge, the more confidence you will feel. Do your homework.

- Be simple in your communication. Joseph Priestley put it this way, "The more elaborate our means of communication, the less we communicate." There is so much truth to this statement. And one way to make complex subjects simple is to use common objects to teach complex principles.

For example, I once had to do a presentation to a nonprofit organization that was searching for a bank to manage its investments. We had reams of material for them to review, complete with historical investment performance charts, statistics, and a complex analysis. But the decision-makers at the nonprofit, to whom we would be making the presentation, had limited knowledge regarding investments. They were each local community members with backgrounds in public education, not in investments.

So instead of using reams of material, we used three crayons—each of a primary color. We then told the group that in making their decision there are three primary concerns they should consider—safety, simplicity, and return on investment. Because we communicated to them using concepts they could understand, they chose us to provide the services. Be simple in your communication.

- Finally, speak from your heart. This implies that you must believe what you are saying and that you should be living the principles you are teaching. In essence, you must be the message you are delivering. Speak from your heart.

Public speaking can be frightening, but it can be rewarding. Doing your part ahead of time will help reduce the jitters and lead to greater enjoyment.

Invitation to Act

The next time you are called on to speak publicly, do your homework, be simple in your communication, and speak from your heart.

What are your thoughts, feelings, and impressions?

58

The Power of Patience

In today's fast-food, get-it-done-now pace of life, there is an increasing need for all of us to recognize the power of patience. Patience, as we all know, is a virtue. It is one of those virtues that we expect of others, but often exempt ourselves from possessing. In the words of Bill McGlashen, "Patience is something you admire in the driver behind you, but not in the one ahead."

In that spirit, a quick review of the principle of patience may be of benefit to all of us. And the truth is, there are at least three distinct kinds of patience: patience with others, patience with process, and patience with self.

Patience with others honors the agency, the capabilities, and the circumstances of those around us. Not everyone moves as quickly or does all that we might expect. But patience allows understanding to precede accusation. The clerk at the supermarket checkout line who seems to be moving slowly may have just lost a loved one, and the distracted driver in the car in front of you may have just received some traumatic news. Whatever the situation may be, a little bit of patience goes a long way.

Patience with process is also a virtue that yields results. Besides, many things in life just can't be hurried. A seed will germinate at its own rate. You can water it all you want, but nature marches to its own drumbeat. The same is true with the maturity process of a child. Each blossoms according to a unique timeline. And any effort to force growth, whether in plants or humans, can lead to frustration, discouragement, and, in some cases, damage.

Patience with ourselves is often one of the most difficult pills to swallow. We are all our own worst critics, and we routinely expect ourselves to perform our functions in life on a flawless basis—particularly when we compare ourselves to others. However, we all need to remember that most good things take time, and we are often least inclined to give ourselves the time we need to do and become what we desire.

Patience, however, does not mean sitting idly by. Rather it implies doing all we can and not giving up, even when the results come slowly.

No matter what we are dealing with, a lack of patience normally leads to an increase in anger and, quite often, a loss of temper. Then the productivity of patience is replaced with the debilitating effects of a lack thereof. In the words of Arnold H. Glasgow, we should always remember that "you get the chicken by hatching the egg, not by smashing it."

Whatever your situation or your circumstances, remember the power of patience. Work hard, be steady, and, whether dealing with others, with processes, or with yourself, be patient.

Invitation to Act

The next time you are tempted to be impatient with someone else, a process, or yourself, take a breath, think it through, and decide to be patient.

What are your thoughts, feelings, and impressions?

59

On Your Mark, Get Set . . .

Picture this: The runners are in place, their positions are set, and their muscles are toned, trained, and poised to explode into action. Then come the awaited words, "On your mark, get set"—and the gun goes off, releasing the runners to sprint toward the finish line.

But nobody moves.

Each runner remains at their post, feet firmly placed against the block. And the race is never run. The preparation, the anticipation, and the expectation of triumph are washed away by a wave of inaction.

Unfortunately, life is filled with "un-run" races. Plans are made, but never implemented. Dreams fill our hearts but are never converted into reality. Good intentions pave our highways, but we fail to travel down them. We learn, we think, we hope, but we do not act. Johann Wolfgang von Goethe, the great German author, put it this way: "Knowing is not enough; we must apply. Willing is not enough; we must do."

Doing converts energy to action and turns vision into victory. It brings life into our lives and breathes hope into hopeless situations. Indeed, we are happiest, it seems, when our hands are busy and our lives are engaged in doing something.

So often we think and speak of great things to come, but then we don't act on our good intentions.

Why don't we act, why don't we do? Perhaps we feel that our action may be inconsequential. What if Rosa Parks had not done what she did when she refused to give up her seat on the bus? What if Helen Keller had not acted on her desire to learn to communicate? What if our founding forebears had dreamed of liberty but had never put pen to paper in framing and signing the Declaration of Independence?

Fear is often another reason for not acting. Fear of failure, fear of criticism, fear of the unknown. And the truth is there is risk in acting and doing. But, as H. Jackson Brown stated, "Don't be afraid to go out on a limb. That's where the fruit is." When we are resolved to do something, knowing in our heart that it is right, fear can be replaced with courage and a willingness to do hard things.

Whatever our reasons for not doing may be, success in any realm always comes to those who act and do something. Mark Twain explained, "There are basically two types of people. People who accomplish things, and people who claim to have accomplished things. The first group is less crowded."

Decide today to do. Plan to act. Choose to be part of the group of people who accomplish things by overcoming fears and acting. Now, on your mark, get set. GO.

Invitation to Act

This one is simple. Pick one area where you have an impression to do something. Stop thinking about it and go do it now.

What are your thoughts, feelings, and impressions?

60

Time to Say Goodbye

This is the sixtieth chapter of the book, and it is the last. Throughout the previous fifty-nine chapters I have had the privilege of sharing a few thoughts with you about building your road to remarkable, and it has been one of the most rewarding endeavors of my life.

I cannot adequately express my gratitude to all who contributed to this book—and to my life—from birth to today. Nor can I fully convey my appreciation to you for having taken the time to read it.

"Time to Say Goodbye" is not only a prelude to a farewell, but also the title of a beautiful song performed by the world-renowned tenor, Andrea Bocelli. It is a romantic, inspiring work, and it is one of my favorites.

The phrase, "time to say goodbye," has the potential of conjuring up much emotion. Said to a child who wants to stay and play, it is the source of disappointment. Said to a spouse, a parent, a child, or a friend leaving for an extended tour of duty—military or otherwise—it is the source of renewed expressions of love and a hope for a quick and safe return. Said by someone who stands on death's doorstep, to someone they love, it inspires the deepest, most sacred emotions that are both indescribable and unfathomable. Goodbyes are never easy.

Yet, in every goodbye, there is opportunity for growth. This is true not only in the case of saying goodbye to some*one* (where absence makes the heart grow fonder) but in saying goodbye to some*thing*.

For example, at age twelve, Andrea Bocelli suffered a head injury during a soccer game and lost his sight. In so doing he said goodbye to the gift of vision but welcomed the blossoming of his gift of music that has now touched the world. When one door in life closes, another one seems to open.

Likewise, each time we say goodbye to a bad habit, we make room for the creation of a good one. And each time we crush one of our weaknesses, we can simultaneously build our strength. Life is a continual journey of saying goodbye to the old and welcoming the new. The process of growing, moving forward, changing, and becoming more than we are is always painful, but always worth it.

And the truth is, we do not make this journey alone. We are surrounded by friends and loved ones whose influence both inspires us and gives us the strength to say our goodbyes. The richest blessings in our lives come from the people we love and the people who love us. They are the gems of our lives whose existence inspires, lifts, comforts, and gives purpose to all that we do. And they are those who have inspired the topics and the stories contained in these sixty chapters. To each of them, and to all of you, I extend my heartfelt gratitude.

I hope you will return to these pages often, looking for an idea, a spark of inspiration, or a gentle nudge to take one step forward in some area of your life. I wish you the very best as you continue your journey, building your road to remarkable one brick at a time. Now, at least for the moment, it's time to say goodbye.

Invitation to Act

The next time you say goodbye to anyone or anything, take time to appreciate what you have learned, experienced, and felt. Then walk through the opening door of opportunity on your road to remarkable.

What are your thoughts, feelings, and impressions?

Acknowledgments

A painting is the sum of thousands of brush strokes. In like manner, this book is the product of innumerable influences in my life. While I may have put pen to paper, those whose lives intersected with mine contributed the experiences, the lessons, the stories, the examples, and the pearls of wisdom that form the fabric of what has been written. To mention them all would be like naming the stars in the sky. Yet, in every heavenly expanse, there are those celestial bodies whose light somehow shines so brightly as to merit special recognition.

Bob Quinn, Thom Nielsen, John Whetten, Lyle Cottle, Steve Futrell, and Doug Kapnick are cherished friends and associates whose example and instruction inspired and shaped my career and my life. Thank you for teaching me by word and example, and by always telling me the truth with love.

The employees at Citizens Bank, Bank One, the Bank of Lenawee, Monarch Community Bank, and Chemical Bank inspired me to write the chapters of this book—and many more. Working and serving with you was an honor and a delight.

Ms. Mildred Webster, my high school English teacher, insisted on excellence, tolerated our adolescence, and never stopped believing that we could learn. Thank you for the price you paid to set our thoughts free through the gift of language.

Sandra Wendel, my trusted editor and new friend, helped me find the statue in the marble and chip off the rough edges.

Finally, but most importantly, I acknowledge the brightest stars in the greatest constellation of my life—my family.

To my mom, Barbara DeVries, thank you for painting pictures of love with your words of wisdom. You have taught me to love writing and to cherish selfless acts of kindness.

To my dad, Dean DeVries, thank you for showing me how to see beauty in every cloud, glory in every sunset, and optimism in every situation. I have learned from you that things will always work out.

To my brother John, whose memory will never fade. Thank you for a lifetime of boyhood adventures and for your remarkable road that ended far too soon.

To my mother-in-law and father-in-law, Ann Marie and Sherwood Bridges. Thank you for the gift of your precious daughter, for the sewing room and den chats, and for providing an early reading of portions of this manuscript.

To my wife, best friend, and eternal companion, Dyana—thank you for your wit, wisdom, inspiration, intellect, patience, and love. You are the brightest of all the stars in my sky and the reason I wrote this book. Your input and imprint is found on every page, and your influence for good in this world, like the stars, cannot be numbered.

To our children, Heather, Jonathan, Michael, Daniel, Allison, and Andrew—and your incredible spouses—thank you for teaching me the most important lessons in life. Your lives shaped the stories of this book and fill the chapters of my life with joy.

To my grandchildren—sixteen at the time of publishing this book, and all those yet to come—thank you for allowing me another chance to see the magic of life through pure, innocent eyes.

About the Author

Richard J. DeVries spent his career in the banking industry from Dallas to New York City and from Minneapolis to Michigan. He has served as President and CEO of three community banks, has founded two nonprofit organizations, and has served on the board of directors of seventeen nonprofit organizations.

Rick has done public speaking around the country, has authored a newspaper column on leadership and success, and is passionate about identifying, living, and sharing principles that change lives.

He and his wife, Dyana, have been married forty years, have six children, and (at the time of publication) sixteen grandchildren. He is an avid swimmer and skier and occasionally pretends he is a good golfer.